FINDING SUCCESS IN THE HOROSCOPE

Advance Praise

In *Finding Success in the Horoscope,* Jackie Slevin has finally achieved what other books have only attempted. She outlines a clear, logical, and wonderfully workable system that anyone can use to determine the best career path and whether that road to success will be direct or filled with detours. The Slevin System of Horoscope Analysis, as presented here, focuses on the Midheaven—its sign, ruler, aspects to planets, and fixed stars—as well as the Cardinal Axis, which is not usually mentioned in many texts. There are chart examples for every point Slevin makes, and her eye for detail along with her unique style and insights all contribute to a book bound to be a classic. Bravo, Jackie!

—RONNIE GALE DREYER
astrologer, teacher, and author of
Venus Cycles, Vedic Astrology, and *Healing Signs*

FINDING SUCCESS

in the

HOROSCOPE

The Slevin System of Horoscope Analysis

JACKIE SLEVIN

IBIS PRESS
Lake Worth, FL

Published in 2008 by
IBIS PRESS
an imprint of Nicolas-Hays, Inc.
P. O. Box 540206 • Lake Worth, FL 33454-0206
www.nicolashays.com
Distributed to the trade by Red Wheel/Weiser, LLC
65 Parker St., Unit 7 • Newburyport, MA 01950-4600
www.redwheelweiser.com

Library of Congress Cataloging-in-Publication data available on request.

ISBN: 978-0-89254-134-8

VG
Cover and text design by Kathryn Sky-Peck
Cover: A view of the detail in the Astronomical Clock
in Old Town Prague, Czech Republic. Photo by Taylor S. Kennedy,
National Geographic/Getty Images

Printed in the United States of America
12 11 10 09 08 07 06
7 6 5 4 3 2 1

To my mother,
My first astrology teacher,

And my father,
Who taught me to follow through.

TABLE OF CONTENTS

Introduction to the Slevin System
of Horoscope Analysis 1

Chapter 1: Windows on the World: The Midheaven. . . . 7

Chapter 2: Location is Everything:
The Principal Planet 41

Chapter 3: Dignities, Mutual Receptions, and
Major Configurations. 73

Chapter 4: The Cardinal Axis. 105

Chapter 5: Appearances Count. 117

Chapter 6: It Runs in the Family. 127

Chapter 7: Royal Fixed Stars 137

Chapter 8: The Critical 29th Degree. 157

Chapter 9: The Express Lane to the Top 165

Chapter 10: And for the Rest of Us 183

Epilogue 191

Notes 193

List of Charts 197

About the Author 198

ACKNOWLEDGMENTS

My heartfelt thanks go out to the members of the New Jersey chapter of the National Council for Geocosmic Research (NCGR), who encouraged me to expand a lecture into a book; the late, great Lois Rodden, who encouraged me to write and whose Astrodatabank provides my stock in trade; the late Frances McEvoy, who shone the light at the end of the tunnel; and, most of all, my husband, Pat, and sons Patrick, John, and Dan. You sustain me.

Introduction to the Slevin System of Horoscope Analysis

Success is a science.
If you have the conditions, you get the result.

Oscar Wilde

Horoscope analysis is by turns infinitely vast and minutely intricate. The myriad placements and interactions among planets, angles, and houses create a labyrinth of cosmic design to illustrate, illuminate, and ultimately guide us through the journey of life. The complexity of the design, however, is that horoscope interpretation is imminently wide open to speculation on topics ranging from obscure mythological correlation to the accurate timing of events. The word "horoscope" is derived from the Latin *horos scopus*, or "picture of the hour." Thus a horoscope is a specialized picture of planets, a *map*, nothing more, and nothing less. Successful navigation of a map is contingent upon determining direction. The most commonly known instrument used for the purpose is a compass, in which a magnetic needle is freely suspended so that the earth's magnetic field turns to align itself with a specific point. To the navigator, this specific point is True North. To the astrologer, it is the Midheaven.

This summit of the horoscope defines who we are when functioning at our highest level, when we are the heroes of our own lives. Simply put, our Sun sign defines who we are, the

Moon sign defines what we need, and the sign on the Ascendant defines how our personality is presented to the world at large. The sign on the Midheaven, however, defines what we are trying to *reach*, what we're striving for, and how we find our place in the world. It does not, however, describe our conditions on the journey to our personal destination, or whether our climb will be enabled in a chair lift or we undergo superhuman labors to reach the top. Nor does it instruct us how to reach the summit or the supplies required for the climb. In order to reach our own personal peak of achievement, each of us needs the necessary equipment, a map, and a method. Our horoscope is the map. Planets in aspects to the Midheaven describe the equipment. *The 12-Step Slevin System is a new method of navigation.*

The development of skill is bred into the human condition and reaches across both ancient and modern civilizations. The proverb, "Give me a fish and I eat for a day, teach me to fish and I eat for a lifetime" is a common theme in career and vocational guidance. Taking this wisdom to a higher level yields another proverb: "Give a man a rod and he's a fisherman. Give him a boat and now he's a businessman." What transformed the simple fisherman to a businessman was that, using his boat, he discovered a method to move the fish, transferring them from the deep to the marketplace. *He moved the goods.*

The purpose of this book is to illustrate breakthrough techniques that utilize aspects to the Midheaven and other subtle planetary symbolism to help determine how individuals can find their own True North by defining their abilities, developing their talents, gaining the highest visibility, and ultimately attaining success. In short, *how to transfer your own goods from low visibility to high visibility.* Moreover, it takes a new look at ancient methods of delineation and applies them to target career potential. Using only the natal chart as the barometer of potential and visibility, and the Success Formula, *Finding Success in the Horoscope* illustrates new techniques of delineation. It uses aspects to the Midheaven to define the "boat," or the method of navigation in each person's chart to transfer their goods from the raw materials of talent to the center of the public marketplace.

Whether one works as a fisherman, plumbing the murky deep for its bounty, or as a software engineer, coding complex computer programs, the application of skill determines one's success in everyday living. While there is no single planet or angle in the horoscope named *skill, talent,* or *career,* subtle, often hidden intricacies of delineation can access a common thread to join these precious nouns together to produce the desired result. Obscure indicators often effect a hand-in-glove fit to complete the jigsaw puzzle, thus maneuvering the compass needle to our own True North.

Webster's Unabridged Dictionary defines success as "the favorable or prosperous termination of attempts or endeavors." In short, success crowns the efforts that produce a desired result. Success, however, does not necessarily imply financial success. The desired result from attempts or endeavors could be a world away from a hefty paycheck. Mother Theresa was extremely successful at helping the poorest of the poor, yet earning a high income was not her motivation. She simply utilized her Midheaven, her point of highest visibility, to achieve her desired result. Humanitarian Simon Wiesenthal spent decades searching for Nazi officials to bring them to trial for their atrocious crimes against humanity, yet his income was not connected to his vocation and had little bearing on his achievement. Achievement in career endeavors does not necessarily co-exist with financial reward. Old textbooks of astrology use the Midheaven to determine an individual's rank. Whether rank is a birthright or a desired result, it does not describe cash flow. Nor is birth or social rank implemented in democratic societies where bettering oneself is an inalienable right. Following our bliss is the very stuff of life, liberty, and the pursuit of happiness. Money is the gravy, and gravy needs to be passed around. The tangible by-products of success can be shared, but the recipients don't share the success of the donor. Bliss, like beauty, is in the eye of the beholder, and beholding is wholly dependent upon one's point of view, which is always most desirable at the highest possible vantage point. The Midheaven is the highest point of the horoscope, and thus where one shines at their brightest.

The Slevin System is in no way the be-all and end-all of horoscope interpretation. It does not solve relationship problems or predict events. It does, however, offer a step-by-step shorthand method of horoscope interpretation that uses Occam's razor to define optimum professional potential, one's own True North, and highlights the most effective itinerary to fulfillment and success, including alternate routes. The Slevin System will benefit anyone interested in defining successful and attainable career goals, from the astrological neophyte to the professional astrologer. This unique method has not been published anywhere else, and revolutionizes astrological career counseling.

Finding Success in the Horoscope uses birth data from Lois Rodden's Astrodatabank and from friends and clients using the Rodden Rating System for accuracy.

All charts are presented in the Placidus house system.

Only the natal horoscope is used in this system. Maps become embellished as territory develops over time, but True North remains constant despite climate change and atmospheric pressure. The same can be said for the horoscope and the Midheaven. While progressed charts, solar arcs, and other techniques illustrate turns of events and are strategic components of predictive astrology, they are abstractions stemming from the matrix of the natal horoscope. Potential, ability, and skill are shown in the natal chart, along with inclination and temperament. These raw materials of personality must be defined, developed, and directed to crown our efforts and produce the desired result.

Imagine the components of the natal horoscope as puzzle pieces of the personality that have been spread out, ready to be assembled into their correct positions. The Slevin System is a new and unique method of fitting them together to achieve completion of the Big Picture.

Enjoy the process, and once you've determined your best route to the summit, enjoy the view. It's lovely at the top.

The 12-Step Slevin System

1. Determine the sign and degree on the Midheaven (MC).

2. Find the planet nearest to that degree in Ptolemaic aspect within signs. This is the Principal Planet.

3. Note any planets in the tenth house.

4. Note the Principal Planet's sign and strength, whether in dignity or debility, and direction, whether direct, retrograde, or stationary.

5. Note the house in which the Principal Planet is posited or whether it is within 5 degrees of the next house cusp.

6. Determine the aspects the Principal Planet makes.

7. Note the house (or houses) this planet rules.

8. Note if the Principal Planet is exactly conjunct or within one degree of the Cardinal Axis.

9. Note if the Principal Planet is in mutual reception or mixed mutual reception with any other planets.

10. Note if the Principal Planet is exactly conjunct or within one degree of Royal Fixed Stars.

11. Combine the above factors (where applicable) to discover the most definitive shorthand description of the personality, and define the strongest attributes for achieving success, notoriety, or the highest visibility.

12. Repeat this process with the planet nearest to the degree of the Principal Planet.

The Principal Planet is the key significator to determining the path of least resistance to achievement. An exact trine of Mercury to the Midheaven is more inclined to produce someone who excels in the mercurial occupations of writing, reporting, or clerical work than merely having Mercury prominent in the horoscope or a Gemini Midheaven.

The Midheaven is one's personal marketplace, where one travels to display their wares in high visibility for trade or merely to dress up and present themselves to the public at large. As the fisherman transported his fish to the market stall that specifically sold fish, so every individual needs to present their goods, whether in a basic, unadorned window or draped in pomp and circumstance. With few exceptions, most people have had the experience of being visible in a marketplace, whether it's running an errand to the row of shops on Main Street or negotiating a corporate merger in a high-rise in Times Square. *The presentation of one's self to the public at large is the key to achieving high visibility.*

The sign on the Midheaven describes our personal marketplace, or our state of public presentation. Let us now go to the market to review what each sign on the Midheaven has to present.

Chapter One

WINDOWS ON THE WORLD—
THE MIDHEAVEN

*Grace is given of God, but knowledge
is bought in the market.*
ARTHUR HUGH CLOUGH

As with any puzzle, it's best to begin with the corner pieces, to determine the angles on the frame.

The crux of the Slevin System in horoscope analysis lies in the determination of one's skills and how those skills will be made visible to others and to the world at large. The fundamental premise is learning how to achieve success, notoriety, status, or the highest visibility utilizing aspects and other techniques. These are largely dependent on the Midheaven (MC) and the Ascendant, the angles of perspective, our personal windows on the world.

Across the globe of twenty-four time zones and approximately 120 degrees of latitude, over 15,000 babies are born every hour. The planets in their horoscopes are essentially identical, with the exception of the Moon, which changes every two hours, and the angles, which change every four minutes. Thus the angles of the horoscope are crucial in determining personal distinctiveness from collective similarity.

People Live What They See

The Ascendant is the window or lens through which we project our personality. It defines the point where we emerge from birth into the world and thus describes our physical appearance and the conditioning of our early life. The sign on the Ascendant, planets conjunct it or in the first house, cast a permanent veil of influence over this window, while planets in the first house serve as continuous window dressing. Planets in aspect to the Ascendant also play their role in the native's perspective, for they describe what the native first notices when he or she looks out of this window. *The ascendant and the planets in aspect to it describe the circumstances and environment of one's personal presentation.* This angle, and the window treatment it receives, will determine whether one's personal window on the world is perceived through a glass darkly or through a vista of spectacular brilliance.

The Midheaven, or MC, is our window on the world at large. Here we shine the brightest, attain our highest and greatest perspective, and display our public presentation. The planet ruling the MC describes our view of the world, *our personal peak of achievement.* Serving as the principal indicator of one's aspirations, position in life, status, reputation, and rank, it is defined in modern terms as the career or profession. Using either the ancient or modern perspective, it is the crown of the chart, the pinnacle of our achievements, and it serves as the guidepost to where our life's purpose is consummated. *The Midheaven and the planets in aspect to it describe the circumstances and environment of one's public presentation. Planets in aspect to the Midheaven describe the equipment needed to climb the mountain to our highest destination. Aspects to the Midheaven describe the journey.*

Aries Midheaven—Ruling Planet: Mars

The Aries stall in the marketplace is one that is fast-paced and loaded with constant action. Spontaneity is more valuable than the tried and true, and their stall will be guarded covetously as

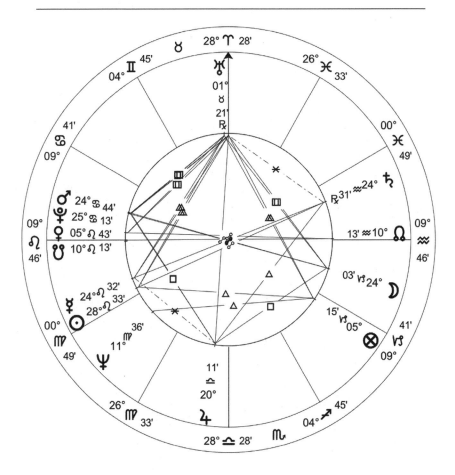

Chart 1. Aries Midheaven: General Norman Schwarzkopf, August 22, 1934, 4:45 AM EDT Trenton, NJ 40N14, 74W46.

new trails are blazed for prospective venues of their innovative presentations. Self-sufficient in the extreme, they are disinclined to share their place in the limelight or take direction from anyone. Raw energy is their stock in trade, and here is where a shopper finds soldiers, athletes, pioneers, explorers, hunters, leaders, daredevils and self-made, rugged individualists. The heat is on in this stall, and working with fire, knives, sharp tools, or anything dangerous for that matter, creates intrigue and gives the Aries Midheaven the knife-edge challenge they need to promote, chase, or conquer. They're no strangers to hard, physical work and competition of any kind is their clarion call to battle.

Chart 1 on page 9, an example of Aries on the Midheaven, is American military general Norman Schwarzkopf, who, in August 1990, executed Operation Desert Storm, the U.S. led campaign that liberated Kuwait during the Persian Gulf War. Commanding the respect, admiration, and affection of an entire nation, "Stormin' Norman" Schwarzkopf was a veteran of numerous military assignments, including two tours of duty of Vietnam and, in 1983, as commander of U.S. forces in the invasion of Grenada. The son of a West Point graduate and general by the same name, Schwarzkopf was bred to soldiering from his early youth. After attending his father's alma mater, he later earned a master's degree in Engineering, specializing in guided missiles. Disgusted by the military tactics of the Vietnam War and their attendant corruption, Schwarzkopf, convinced that the system could only change by good soldiers rising to the top, internalized this lesson when running his combat units in the Persian Gulf. As a result, casualties were minimal, the Saudi culture was respected, and troops were treated with dignity. With his advice to others as "Be the leader you would like to have," Schwarzkopf retired from active duty in 1991. His autobiography *It Doesn't Take a Hero* was published in 1992.

Taurus Midheaven—Ruling Planet: Venus

The Taurus stall is likely placed front and center in the market, for Taurus is the sign of the bank, the very cornerstone of business, and the teller is always present to exchange currency and cash checks. Moving the merchandise and maintaining a positive cash flow is the raison d'être, and music and arts and crafts are just as crucial to Taurus Midheaven as the coin of the realm. They seek to present the public with a garden of earthly delights, celebrating Mother Nature in all her glory. Here is the creature comfort zone, the place to buy perfume, flowers, musical instruments and artists' supplies, along with agricultural products.

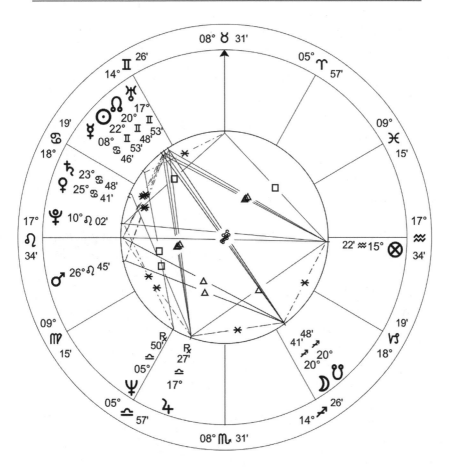

Chart 2. Taurus Midheaven: Donald Trump, June 14, 1946, 9:51 AM EDT Queens, NY, 40N43, 73W52.

This stall is the meeting place for speculating businesspeople, bankers, insurance brokers, musicians, singers, sculptors, artists, gardeners, farmers, naturalists, and cowboys. The acquisition of legal tender to fertilize fields for new growth is standard operating procedure for these folks, who seek a comfortable routine to sow and reap for a high rate of return. Sensual, possessive, and deliberate, they know you get what you pay for.

Chart 2, for American entrepreneur Donald Trump, provides an example of Taurus Midheaven. Trump is a world-renowned real estate tycoon who owns some of the world's most prestigious addresses including The Trump Palace, Trump Parc, Trump Plaza, and the Trump World Tower. One of the richest men in the world, Trump, the son of a self-made millionaire in real estate development, accompanied his father to building sites in youth. After graduating from New York Military Academy, Fordham University, and first in his class at the Wharton School of Business, Trump was welcomed into his father's real estate team, the Trump Organization, and gravitated toward New York's most affluent clubs, speculating and investing his way up. Known as the P.T. Barnum of real estate, Trump makes a bold statement in person, in the press, and in public, stamping his name on each building with his Midas touch. Overextended at age 40, his empire began to decline and fall when he was unable to pay $8.8 billion in loans. Through trading and leveraging, he restructured his colossal debt, hitting the jackpot again with investing in the Trump Taj Mahal, a deluxe gambling casino in Atlantic City, New Jersey, and waterfront property in Brooklyn, New York. Trump's toys include a yacht worth $100 million and a 118-room palace in Florida. The author of three books, *The Art of the Deal* (1987), *Surviving at the Top* (1990), and *The Art of the Comeback* (1997), the potentate's byline is, "I like thinking big. If you're going to be thinking, you might as well think big."

Gemini Midheaven—Ruling Planet: Mercury

This stall is the information center, complete with the post office, telephone, Internet access, and newsstand. Bulletin boards are available for posting messages, and here is where to use the public address system. This is where you hail a taxi, send a telegram, wire a transfer, and connect to the public transportation system. Pens, paper, postcards, paperbacks, and magazines of all kinds are for sale here, and this is where to rent or purchase an automobile, bicycle, Ipod, beeper, cell phone, or radio. A variety of foreign languages are spoken and if you need a

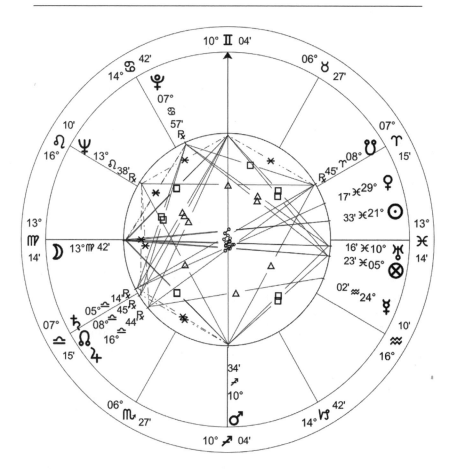

Chart 3. Gemini Midheaven: Jack Kerouac March 12, 1922, 6:00 PM EST, Lowell, MA 42N38, 71W19.

translation of anything, from Sanskrit, Shakespeare, or the latest lingo, you came to the right place. The Gemini stall is abuzz with communicators of all kinds, including journalists, reporters, couriers, teachers, writers, sales representatives, telephone operators, drivers, radio announcers, auctioneers, merchants, traders, receptionists, commuters, public relation specialists, commentators, gossips, forgers, and con artists. These multifaceted individuals in this stall usually pursue more than one career. Moving with the speed of light, Gemini rules flexibility, motion, dexterity, and agility of wit as well as body. Acrobats, comedians and dancers dwell here, too.

An example of Gemini Midheaven is seen in Chart 3 on page 13, American writer and poet Jack Kerouac. Author of the classic *On the Road,* the definitive bible of the Beat generation, Jean-Louis Lebris de Kerouac was the son of French Canadian immigrants and spoke English as a second language in his formative years. He enlisted in the merchant marines in 1939 after graduating high school, followed by a brief stint in the navy. In 1945 he met his mentor, lover and traveling buddy Neal Cassady, the model of the character Dean Moriarty, with whom he spent three years roaming America. By 1950 he published his first novel of his Lowell boyhood, *Town and the City.* The following year he wrote his first draft of *On the Road* on a single roll of butcher paper in three weeks.

Between 1952–1956, Kerouac resumed his peripatetic life of roaming North America and Mexico, supporting himself with odd jobs, studying and rewriting *On the Road*, and other experimental works, in his own compositional method of "spontaneous prose." The publication of *On the Road* in 1957 was an overnight sensation, firmly establishing Kerouac as the mouthpiece of the Beatniks. Additional novels *The Subterraneans* and *Dharma Bums* followed one year later.

Disillusioned with fame and its resultant loss of privacy, Kerouac attempted to withdraw from notoriety in California, where, in 1960, he published *Big Sur*, a soul-searching narrative of his struggle with alcoholism, the disease that ultimately caused his death on October 13, 1969.

Cancer Midheaven—Ruling Planet: The Moon

Here is the customer service center. The family-owned and operated restaurant and inn is located in this stall, where you restore and nourish yourself with chicken soup for the body and for the soul. Cancer provides, nurtures, and protects from womb to tomb, and catering to the public is the highest priority. The three most fundamental needs—food, clothing, and shelter—are available in abundance. The national flag is proudly displayed, tradition is upheld and observed, and Mom and Pop of this establishment are local legends of hospitality. They preside as chieftains of an extended clan of solid citizens who stick together; family members who work here have a job for life, those who don't feel Mom's apron strings pulling them home. The all-consuming family bond can extend beyond blood ties to embrace the human family at large. In addition to the solace of home and hearth, the Cancer stall offers care-givers of all kinds, women's commodities, babies, midwives, nurses, chefs, bakers, insurance brokers, restaurant owners, innkeepers, photographers, shopkeepers, grocers, brewers, vintners, fishermen, sailors and ship captains. Historians and keepers of the oral tradition are held in the highest esteem here. The Moon rules sensation, response, the ebb and flow of the public, tempo and rhythm. Dancers and musicians and entertainers are found here, too.

Chart 4 on page 16, Simon Wiesenthal, shows an example of a Cancer Midheaven. Wiesenthal was a Polish architect and author of *The Murderers Among Us* (1967), his memoir of tracking down members of the Nazi regime who were responsible for the Holocaust. After receiving a degree in architectural engineering in 1932, Wiesenthal, a Jewish professional, was forced to close his business in 1939 due to the Soviet occupation. Captured in 1941 and assigned to the Osterbahn Works, a forced labor camp, he escaped in October, 1943, weeks before mass annihilation began. Recaptured in 1944, he was sent to Janwska in Lvov, Poland, where, under the advancing Red Army, he was marched under Nazi guard over 400 miles to the Mauthausen concentration camp in Austria. Hovering between life and death, Wiesenthal weighed less than 100 pounds when an American unit liberated the camp on May 5, 1945.

Immediately upon regaining his health, Wiesenthal began gathering evidence on Nazi atrocities for the War Crimes Section of the United States Army, which was utilized in the American

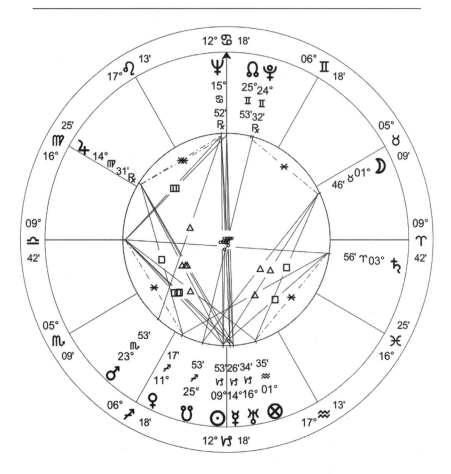

Chart 4. Cancer Midheaven: Simon Wiesenthal. December 31, 1908, 11:30 PM MET, Buczacz, Ukraine 49N04, 25E26

zone war crime trials. In 1947, he opened the Jewish Historical Documentation Center in Linz, Austria, for compiling evidence for future trials. In 1953, Wiesenthal received word that Adolf Eichmann, supervisor of the implementation of the "Final Solution," was seen in Buenos Aires, Argentina. Following a painstaking search and paper trail through Europe, South America, and the Middle East, he eventually brought Eichmann to trial in Israel where he was found guilty of mass murder and executed on May 31, 1961.

Over the next three decades, Wiesenthal and his staff eventually apprehended over 1,100 Nazi war criminals, including Karl Silberbauer, who arrested Anne Frank, Franz Stangl, commandant of Treblinka and Sobibor concentration camps, and, posthumously, the Angel of Death, Josef Mengele.

When once asked to explain his motives for hunting former Nazis along with contemporary neo-Nazis, Wiesenthal replied,

> You believe in God and life after death. I also believe. When we come to the other world and meet millions of Jews who died in the camps and they ask us "What have you done?" there will be many answers. You will say, "I became a jeweler," another will say, "I have smuggled coffee and American cigarettes," another will say "I built houses." But I will say, "I didn't forget you."[1]

Leo Midheaven—Ruler: The Sun

This stall is the grandstand of the market, where performances are held, parades pass, and speeches are given. The local stage is here, where one can view the gamut of performers from street entertainers to Shakespearean productions. There's a recreation center, complete with a playground for children, board and video games, amusement park with rides, gymnasium, gambling casino, and a cabaret with floorshows. The sports arena and racetrack can be found, along with a gym and a spa. This stall houses the gold market and stock exchange, where stocks and commodities are traded with high financial risk. Palatial residences are magnificent, where privileged people rule their empire with an air of command. Catering to the jet set, the cocktail party is at this stall, and the hosts conduct themselves with noblesse oblige. This is the place for romantic trysts, complete with candlelit dinners, midnight moonlight, and champagne breakfasts. It's also the home of the artists' studio, music hall, or any venue for creativity, performing, and display. This stall his home to actors, entertainers, administrators, stock brokers,

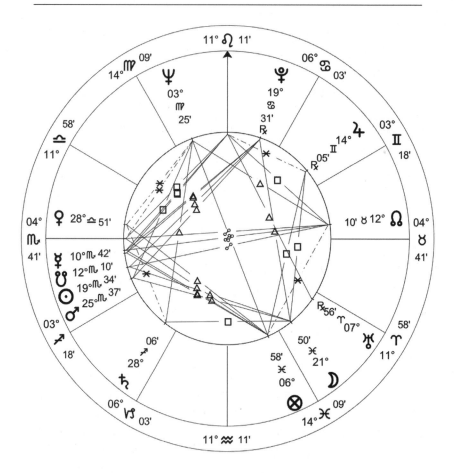

Chart 5. Leo Midheaven: Princess Grace of Monaco, November 12, 1929, 5:31 AM EST, Philadelphia, PA, 39N57, 75W10.

banquet managers, children, coaches, athletes, ambassadors and dignitaries of all kinds. Free-lance bohemians are present, along with artists and pregnant women.

The chart of Grace, Princess of Monaco, shown as Chart 5, is an example of Leo Midheaven.

Princess Grace, born Grace Patricia Kelly, was an Academy-Award winning American actress. Grace Kelly, a shy, convent-educated girl barely out of her teens, was a Hollywood sensation in the films *High Noon, Rear Window, High Soci-*

ety, Dial M for Murder, and *To Catch a Thief.* Her mysterious combination of sex appeal edged with propriety earned her the nickname, "The Pious Man's Marilyn Monroe." She was the number one box office hit in 1954 and received more fan mail than anyone at MGM studios, eventually winning the Academy Award for Best Actress for *The Country Girl* in 1955. While attending the Cannes Film Festival later that year, she met Prince Rainier of Monaco, who was taken by her charm and beauty. Accepting his proposal of marriage to her six months later, her marriage vows transformed into Her Serene Highness, Princess of Monaco. Her royal wedding was the first media social event to be televised. The fairy-tale princess lived in the ancestral Rainier castle and gave birth to three royal children. An committed philanthropist, Princess Grace founded a school in Monaco for aspiring artists, established the Princess Grace awards for excellence in young dancers, actors, and filmmakers, was President of the American Red Cross, and gave much of her time to improving the lives of the Monegasques. Despite her royal status, she was trapped by the pressure of living in the public eye, constantly surrounded by reporters and photographers, and was singularly unprepared for the fundamental cultural differences between her and Prince Rainier, who shared none of her interests in the arts. Drifting apart from her husband in the '70s, yet keeping up appearances, Princess Grace moved to Paris with her two daughters. On September 13, 1982, Princess Grace suffered a stroke while driving, careening her car off a cliff and crashing 120 feet below. She died of her injuries the following day.

Virgo Midheaven—Ruling Planet: Mercury

The Virgo stall may not be a grandiose grandstand or a garden of earthly delights, but no one can be without it. In short, this is the stall of fundamental necessities for the daily grind. This is where you'll find the drug store, doctor's and dentist's office, food market, bakery, health food store, and nutritionist. Everything

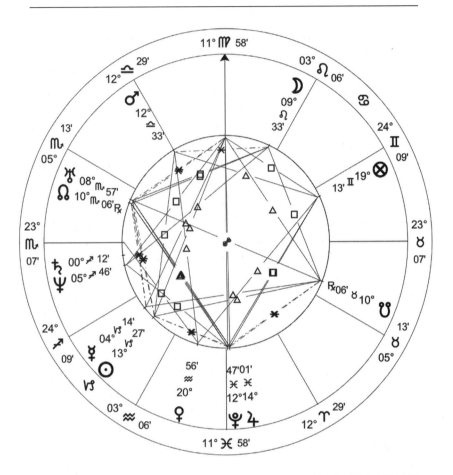

Chart 6. Virgo Midheaven: Louis Braille, January 4, 1809, 4:00 AM LMT, Coupvray, France, 48N54 002E48.

for your pet is here, including the veterinarian. Look no further for civic offices, print shop, library, and computer service center, complete with repair shops of all kinds. There are rows of small, quaint stores selling everyday items such as paper, household and office supplies, hardware, software, delicatessens, convenience and candy stores. This stall is peopled with modest, unassuming individuals who work in the service industry and possess practical, specialized, and often scientific skills that require attention to detail. Among them are accountants, bakers, carpenters, cooks, civil servants, clerks, dressmakers, editors, electricians, tailors, librarians, pharmacists, printers, medical professionals of all kinds, mechanics, plumbers, secretaries, receptionists, reservation agents, restaurant servers, tailors, and typists.

An example of Virgo Midheaven is Chart 6, French inventor and educator Louis Braille .

Blinded at the age of 3 in an accident, Louis Braille, the son of a harness maker, was as outstanding student in the village school despite his handicap. Winning a scholarship to the Royal Institution of Blind Youth in Paris at the precocious age of 10, the ever diligent child learned caning, excelled in oral instruction, and developed his musical talent at the piano and organ. Books at the institute were huge tomes with raised letters of copper wire that needed to be individually traced with the fingertips, a difficult, frustrating process discarded by most students and teachers.

In 1821 Charles Barbier de la Serre, a French army captain, introduced his method of "night writing" to the institute, a code of 12 raised dots allowing soldiers to share secret information on the battlefield in darkness and in silence. The army rejected night writing for being too difficult for soldiers to learn, but 12-year-old Louis was off and running. Streamlining twelve dots down to six dots in different patterns, he adapted the alphabet to this system at 15, and published the first book in Braille at age 20 in 1829. Employed as a teacher and musician in the Institute, the much loved Louis added symbols for math and music in 1837. Public skepticism to "touch reading and writing" was rife, however, and those who wished to learn it did so on their own. After Louis' untimely death of tuberculosis at age 43, a British group, now known as the British Royal Institute of the Blind, implemented his unique system worldwide by 1868.

Universally accepted as the standard system of reading and writing for the blind, Braille has been adapted to nearly every known language. In 1952, the French state finally recognized Louis' remarkable achievement and interred his body in the Pantheon.

Libra Midheaven—Ruling Planet: Venus

The most obvious feature of this stall is its aesthetic, symmetrical appearance. Perfectly proportioned, it stands out for its atmosphere of elegance and beauty. There are flowers on display and music in the background, and its exquisite décor is replete with pastel colors and artistic flair. Justice and fair play are implemented on a grand scale, for arguing and conflict are not tolerated here. A place of high civility and charm, all its inhabitants are highly adept in the social graces and are strategists for peacemaking. This is where you'll find artists, art dealers, architects, the art museum, beauty salons, cosmetics of all kinds, perfume, fashionable clothing boutique, interior designer, the florist, and jewelry store. Musicians can be found here, particularly those who harmonize the melody line. If you need to solve a dispute this stall provides impartial mediators, referees, marriage counselors, negotiators, and divorce lawyers. Contracts of all kinds are written here, along with pre- and post-nuptial agreements. This is the stall of partnerships, whether marriage, live-in, or business, and its opposite end of opponents and enemies.

Chart 7, that of French actress, singer, activist Brigitte Bardot, presents an example of Libra Midheaven. The daughter of an engineer and a homemaker, young Brigitte was encouraged to study dance and music, and proved to be quite adept at both. A natural beauty, she was the cover girl for Elle magazine at 15 where film director Roger Vadim discovered her, marrying her three years later. Casting her in *And God Created Woman* in 1956, she launched her career as "the French sex kitten," becoming the main topic of conversation in 47 percent of French households by 1960. One of the highest paid French actresses of the '60s, she was known not only for films such as *La Vérité* (1960) and *Le Mépris* (1963), but Bardot also recorded several pop songs that skyrocketed on the French charts. As the archetypal femme fatale, she was hounded by the press and the paparazzi for her preternatural sexuality, her sizzling love life on and off camera, her multiple

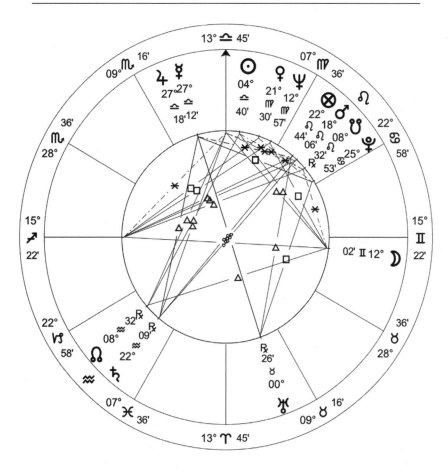

Chart 7. Libra Midheaven: Brigitte Bardot, September 28, 1934, 1:15 PM BST -1:00, Paris, France 48N52, 2E20.

marriages, suicide attempts, and the giving up of her son to be raised by relatives. Described as a force of nature, Bardot's siren song of seduction lived up to the title every time.

Leaving acting in 1973, volatile superstar Bardot became an avid animal rights activist and a recluse. Purchasing a farm outside Paris, she fiercely protects her privacy, along with her forty cats, dozen dogs, and assorted livestock, most of which were saved from the animal pound or butcher's block. Setting a record as the most ardent celebrity of animal rights, Bardot speaks out on the cruelty against whales, seals, donkeys, sheep, and wolves. A committed vegetarian, she was the first French person to publicly denounce the barbaric methods of slaughtering animals for food, getting a bill passed that a stun gun be used to eliminate unnecessary suffering, and won a prohibition against the sale of baby seal fur. Claiming that in her salad days she was the hunted animal, she empathizes with their plight.

Bardot published her autobiography, *Initials B.B.* in 1996. Shunning cosmetic surgery, she has preferred to age naturally with dignity, and is the most noted European celebrity in the cause against cruelty to animals.

Scorpio Midheaven—Ruler Mars and Pluto

This stall has an air of mystery about it, for it's a place of hidden agendas. Its eerie décor beckons with intrigue, yet our instinct warns to proceed with caution, for we get the feeling that we're being watched. And we are. Security cameras are everywhere. This is where we pay taxes and debts, establish credit, apply for loans and invest in bonds. Insurance policies of all kinds can be purchased. It's also the crisis center, where trained therapists can enter and probe the dark corners of the psyche and the soul, and the highly intuitive can perceive the past, present, and future. Not surprisingly, it's the location of the morgue, the funeral parlor, cemetery, and recycling center. Sex is for sale here, and the stall is equipped with secret entrances and exits for stealth and convenience. Underground tunnels and mines lurk beneath, and there's an archeological dig in progress. A science laboratory is here, too, where top-secret research is conducted behind closed doors. Here you'll find gangsters, loan sharks, detectives, research scientists, insurance brokers, tax assessors, security guards, butchers, morticians, psychiatrists, miners, archeologists, astrologers, tarot readers, hypnotists, prostitutes, psychics, surgeons, exterminators, pimps, martial artists, and practitioners of nuclear medicine.

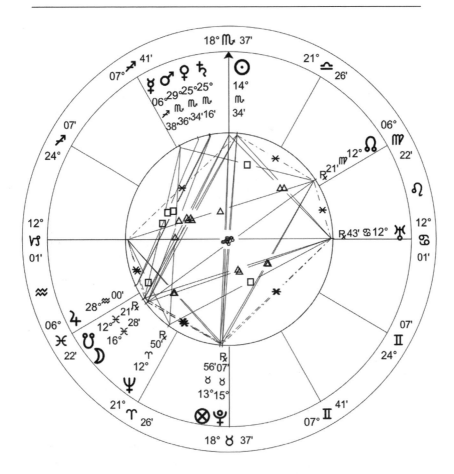

Chart 8. Scorpio Midheaven: Marie Curie, November 7, 1867, 10:36 AM, GMT, Warsaw, Poland, 52N15, 21E00.

An example of Scorpio Midheaven is shown in Chart 8, Polish scientist, physicist, chemist, and author, Marie Curie.

The daughter of two educators, Manya Skladowska was an outstanding student who yearned to attend the University of Warsaw, despite the fact it did not accept females. Her youth ended at age ten when her mother died of tuberculosis. Graduating secondary school at the top of her class at age 15, Manya subsequently suffered a nervous breakdown and was sent to live in rural Poland, which proved to be the only care-free time of her life. Upon recovery, she began tutoring children, a position she held with various families for nine years. Finally accepted to the Sorbonne at age 24, she studied math, physics, and chemistry in French, her second language. Manya was again at the top of her class and, in 1893, she received a master's degree in physics, specializing in the magnetic properties of steel. In the spring of 1894 she earned her second master's degree in mathematics and began searching for laboratory space to work on her research project: measuring the magnetic properties of various steel alloys.

Following a lead, she contacted Pierre Curie at the School of Physics and Chemistry at the University of Paris. Their meeting resulted in love at first sight for Pierre, who, after finding Manya lab space, courted her, affectionately referring to her as Marie in his mother tongue. Their marriage the following year proved to be one of the most extraordinary partnerships in science.

In 1896, working with her husband and friend Henri Becquerel, Marie turned her attention to the recently discovered phenomenon of radiation emission from atoms. For this phenomenon, Marie coined the term "radioactivity." At that time, radioactive waves had just been newly observed, emitting from minerals such as ore, which contain the element uranium. Further investigating uranium rays, Marie found that pitchblende, a uranium-rich mineral, gave off more more radioactivity than could be accounted for by the uranium content alone. She theorized that the pitchblende must contain another strongly radioactive element that had never been detected before. Diligent research led her to the discovery of the elements radium and polonium, with a conclusion that radioactivity was an atomic property and thus had to be present in other elements. After four years of ceaseless work in an unheated shed, Marie and Pierre processed many tons of pitchblende, progressively concentrating the radioactive substances and ultimately extracting centigrams of radium chloride. Their experiments confirmed that diseased, tumor-forming cells were destroyed when exposed to radium. In 1903 they won the Nobel Prize for Physics for the discovery of radioactivity.

Tragically widowed in 1906, Marie went on to take her late husband's post as Chair of Physics at the University of Paris. Continuing her research, Marie won the Nobel Prize for Chemistry in 1911 for isolating pure radium. Among her outstanding achievements was understanding the need to accumulate sources of intense radioactivity to be used for both the treatment of illness and for research in nuclear physics.

During World War I, Marie realized that one form of radiation, X-rays, could be used to save soldiers' lives by enabling doctors view internal bullets, shrapnel, and broken bones. Convincing the French government to allow her to set up the first military radiology centers, she used automobiles converted to vans to transport the X-ray apparatus to the wounded at the battle front. After spending the four years of World War I assisting wounded soldiers, Marie, now frequently ill with the then-unknown perils of radiation poisoning, established Radium Institutes in Warsaw and Paris and became the internationally acknowledged leader in her field. She died of radiation poisoning on July 4, 1934.

Sagittarius Midheaven—Ruling planet: Jupiter

Everything seems to expand here as if viewed through a wide-angle lens, for this is the stall of the Big Picture, where you'll get a bird's-eye view of the world. Entering is similar to crossing a threshold to another realm, for there appear to be no boundaries and foreign languages are heard everywhere. This is the place to pose philosophical questions, where to seek wisdom, develop faith, and have your mind-set challenged and stretched. Chapels, cathedrals, and ashrams are here, where we can witness religious ceremonies and rituals. Here is the airport, where we can travel to distant lands, along with a university, where we can travel in our minds. The court of law is in this stall,

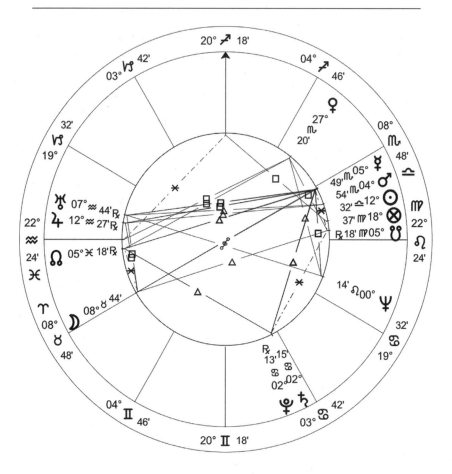

Chart 9. Sagittarius Midheaven: Thor Heyerdahl, October 6, 1914, 4:40 PM MET, Larvik, Norway, 59N04, 10E00.

where justice is administered and ethical issues are presented and discussed. Here you'll find lawyers, priests, nuns, yogis, gurus, pilots, explorers, fundamentalists, philosophers, preachers, professors, scholars, publishers, authors, teachers, and instructors of all kinds. Directors of public relations are seen broadcasting their information and products in as broad a territory as possible and billboards are everywhere, for advertising reigns supreme. People from a vast array of cultures interact in this crossroad of diversity and outreach.

In Chart 9 we see an example of Sagittarius Midheaven. Norwegian sailor, explorer, anthropologist, archeologist, and author, Thor Heyerdahl is known for his unconventional theories on human migration. In 1947, Heyerdahl, a descendant of Vikings, sailed a balsam raft, *Kon Tiki*, across the Pacific from Peru to Polynesia with five companions to prove his thesis that the settlers of Polynesia were of Peruvian origin. He chronicled his adventure in the classic *Kon Tiki* in 1950.

An avid nature lover in youth, Heyerdahl graduated from the University of Oslo with degrees in zoology and geography. Traveling to the Marquesas Islands in Polynesia with his wife in 1937, he was adopted by the Supreme Polynesian Chief of Tahiti and learned the local customs and way of life. Two years later he was living among the Indians of British Columbia at the outbreak of World War II, when he returned to Norway and served with the free Norwegian forces. After the war ended he embarked on his trans-Pacific odyssey, the success of which earned him world-renown, a best-selling book and several awards. In 1952 Heyerdahl led a Norwegian archeological team in a Galapagos expedition, followed by his Easter Island expedition in 1956. This first-ever excavation revealed native Easter Islanders' legends of ancestors coming from far away in the East, along with ancient stone carvings identical to ones in Peru. Heyerdahl's theories of ancient Peruvians migrating to Polynesia were gaining credence.

To prove that ancient Phoenicians could have crossed the Atlantic, the intrepid sailor worked with experts to build a replica of an ancient papyrus boat. Flying a United Nations flag with a crew from seven different nations, the *Ra* was launched from the ancient Phoenician port of Safi in Morocco in 1969, sailing 2700 nautical miles across the widest part of the Atlantic in fifty-six days. Storms and deficiencies in construction necessitated the crew to abandon ship 600 miles from the coast of Barbados. After building another papyrus vessel, Heyerdahl succeeded on his second attempt the following year in the *Ra II*, sailing from Safi to Barbados in fifty-seven days.

The long-held theory that Mediterranean vessels built prior to Columbus could not have crossed the Atlantic was officially overturned.

Heyerdahl sailed a reed raft, the *Tigris* from Iraq to Djibouti in 1977, followed by archeological expeditions in the Maldives in the 1980s. Among his many published works are *Early Man and the Ocean, Ra Expeditions, The Tigris Expedition,* and *The Maldive Mystery.* He died of brain cancer on April 25, 2002.

Capricorn Midheaven—Ruling Planet: Saturn

The chain of command begins right here, for this is the no-nonsense stall of government administration and bureaucracy. The décor is prestigious, conservative, professional, and completely work oriented, with clocks, time cards, and signed photographs of important people. Marble statues, busts, and art of the classical genre are tastefully presented. Furniture is utilitarian, high quality black leather. This is where policy is written, where rank and reputation reign supreme and where careers rise and fall in the public eye. Official notices of all kinds are prominently displayed, including where the line begins to speak to any administrator. The atmosphere is one of strictly business and there is zero tolerance of any infraction of standard office procedure. In this stall of persevering high achievers resides the CEO of the entire marketplace, along with the attendant administrators, board of directors, and all those who possess authority. This is the place to find police officials, judges, surveyors, locksmiths, and all those that set limits and determine boundary lines. Appraisers, diamond merchants, bone surgeons, oral surgeons, and dermatologists are here, too, along with those who deal in anything that confines or contains, such as mold or cast makers, potters, and prosthetic manufacturers. It's also the home of leather and wool merchants, stone and marble cutters, bricklayers and contractors who build foundations to homes, commercial and govern-

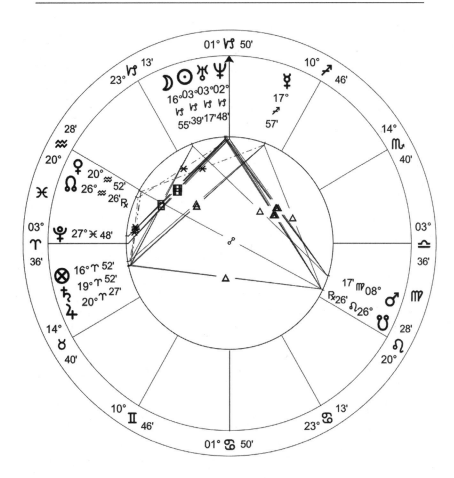

Chart 10. Capricorn Midheaven: Clara Barton, December 25, 1821, 11:40 AM EST Oxford, MA 42N07, 71W51

ment buildings. Living legends dwell here, along with those who become the professional standard against which others are judged and those who persevere against all odds.

Capricorn on the Midheaven is shown in Chart 10, Clara Barton. Founder of the American Red Cross, Clarissa Harlow Barton was the youngest child of farmer Stephen Barton, who had served in the American Revolution under General Anthony Wayne, and feminist Sarah Stone. Raised in a loving family that valued education, Barton was plump, spoke with a lisp, and was painfully shy, but was noticed for her intelligence and capability. At age 15 Barton's parents encouraged her to establish a school for the children of the workers in her brother's saw mill and help nurse the sick. Discovering her self-worth in helping others, Barton capitalized on her small success as a schoolteacher and established the first free public school in Bordentown, New Jersey, increasing enrollment from 6 to 600. When she learned that local officials appointed a male administrator over her, she resigned her position and moved to Washington D.C. in 1853, where she was the first woman in America to hold a government job as a copyist in the patent office. At the outbreak of the Civil War in 1861, Barton began an independent organization to distribute relief and medical supplies to the wounded soldiers from the First Battle of Bull Run. The success of her enterprise earned her a pass to travel with army ambulances to the front lines carrying supplies and nursing the wounded on both Union and Confederate sides for the duration of the war. Known for her humanity and courage under pressure, her work attracted national attention, earning her the nickname "The Angel of the Battlefield."

When the Civil War ended, Barton began the first "Missing Persons Office" in Washington D.C., after she was handed a list of names of soldiers who had died in the Andersonville Confederate prison camp. Traveling to Andersonville, Barton located and marked the graves of thousands of Federal soldiers who died in captivity there and raised the U.S. flag at the dedication of the Andersonville National Cemetery.

Barton's frequent suffering from nervous exhaustion caused her to travel to Geneva, Switzerland, to rest in a sanitarium, where she discovered the International Red Cross. At the outbreak of the Franco-Prussian War in 1870, Barton offered her aid to the Grand Duchess of Baden and organized supplies for the military hospitals. After administering additional relief aid in France, Barton was awarded the Iron Cross by German Emperor William I in 1873.

Returning to the United States, Barton suffered a nervous breakdown that lasted for two years. Upon recovery, she contacted the International Red Cross in Geneva in 1877 and offered to lead an American branch of the organization, beginning a new career at age 56. Her extraordinary efforts led to incorporating the American Red Cross in 1881, with herself as president. During the next decade she personally supervised relief work in over twenty states and Russia, Turkey, and Cuba. A grass-roots organizer and activist of international renown, Barton retired from her beloved Red Cross at age 79. She died of natural causes in Glen Echo, Maryland on April 12, 1912.

Aquarius Midheaven—
Ruling Planets: Saturn and Uranus

This is the virtual stall. Its technological wizardry is state of the art and you need look no further for electronic gadgets, remote units, satellite dishes, and anything pertaining to outer space. Antennae towers are prominent, and there's an aviation center for aircraft construction. Radium and X-ray machines are here, along with radioactivity, uranium, and radar. All activity conducted here is futuristic, and any new or radical idea is heartily championed. This is the stall to search for groups and organizations to join, for everything here is geared toward the common advancement of all humankind. Camaraderie abounds. The wheels and gears of machinery spin to increase production for the masses, and everyone here is a friend you haven't met. Among the people here are those who are a bit off-center, including full-blown eccentrics, free thinkers, astronauts, machinists, inventors, and those who use physics and thermodynamics in their work, such as scientists and engineers. Civil rights activists are everywhere, along with revolutionaries, social reformers, and all those who question authority with bold statements. Here are the movers and shakers in the civic groups that work tirelessly for causes in the community and in the world at large. It's the home for humanitarians

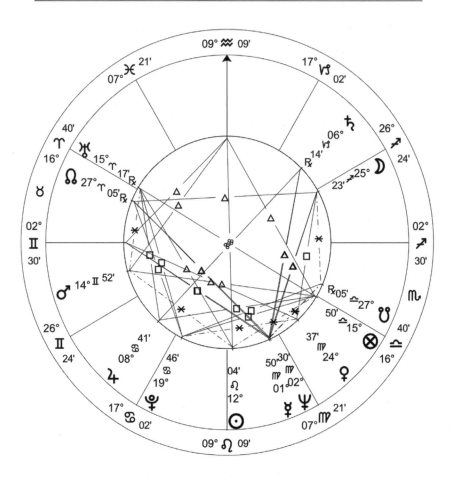

Chart 11. Aquarius Midheaven: Neil Armstrong August 5, 1930, 0:31 AM EST, Washington, OH 40N34, 84W122.

who help on a grand scale and all support groups who share a common bond.

Chart 11 on page 34 provides an example of Aquarius Midheaven. American astronaut and the first man to set foot on the Moon, Neil Armstrong has been an aviation enthusiast since boyhood, when he conducted experiments with model planes in a wind tunnel he created in his parent's basement. Earning a pilot's license at age 16, he graduated from Purdue University in

1955 with a degree in aeronautical engineering. Prior to graduation he served several years of active duty in the U.S. Navy as the youngest pilot in his squadron and was awarded three air medals for flying in combat in the Korean War.

After graduating from college, Armstrong was employed by Lewis Flight Propulsion Laboratory of the National Advisory Committee for Aeronautics (NACA), where he was test pilot for numerous jet aircrafts, including one whose earlier prototype was the first rocket-propelled craft to break the sound barrier. Following acceptance to NASA in 1962, his superior talent earned him enough kudos to immediately begin specialized training. As command pilot for the Gemini 8 mission launched on March 16, 1966, he performed the first successful docking of two vehicles in space. During this mission a malfunction in the manual control board forced Armstrong to bring the airship down in the Pacific. His phenomenal grace under pressure, and his ability to avert potential disaster, led NASA officials to designate him First Command in future space missions. Three years later, he was mission commander of the world's first lunar landing on the Apollo 11, launched on July 16, 1969. Entering the lunar module *The Eagle* on July 20, 1969, the crew separated from the command module to descend approximately three hundred miles to the Moon's surface. At 4:17 PM, EST, they touched down on the Moon in an area known as the Sea of Tranquility. At 10:56 PM, EST, millions around the globe were glued to their television sets as they watched Neil Armstrong step gingerly onto the Moon's surface speaking the historic words, "That's one small step for man, one giant leap for mankind." With fellow astronaut Buzz Aldrin, Armstrong spent over two hours on the Moon, taking photographs and collecting materials from the Moon's surface. Together they planted an American plaque reading "Here men from the planet Earth first set foot upon the Moon. We came in peace for all mankind."

After leaving NASA in 1971, Armstrong was a professor of aerospace engineering at the University of Cincinnati until

1978. He then served as chair for Cardwell International from 1980–1982 and chair for Computing Technologies for Aviation from 1983–1993. Shifting his focus from science to business, in 1997 he became director of Ohio Financial Services, Inc.

Pisces Midheaven—
Ruling Planets: Jupiter and Neptune

This is where to go for quiet time, meditation, solitude, and convalescence. It's the escape route to renew one's self, where one tunes in, turns on, and drops out for whatever reason. There is an ethereal atmosphere of wind chimes, soundscapes, and unusual lighting that acts as a siren song to beckon customers and hold them. Incense is burning to cleanse and purify. Perception becomes enhanced, senses are sharpened, and the responsibilities of everyday life slip away. The bar is in this stall, along with a photographer's dark room and a chemistry lab, where elements blend and converge into other elements. This is where to find the cinema, where moving images in a darkened space are portals to another world. The hospital is located here, along with the jail, orphanage, and cloister. Much activity is conducted behind closed doors, whether for privacy or for stealth. Meetings for Alcoholics Anonymous are here, so is the drug rehabilitation center, halfway house, and family shelter. The open fish market is in this stall, and large animals such as horses and cows will be found here, too. Among the people found in this stall are nuns, monks, ballet dancers, chemists, smugglers, prisoners, those held in any type of bondage, alcoholics, drug addicts, drug and alcohol abuse counselors, drug dealers, secret enemies, spies, the homeless, and indigent people of all types. Welfare recipients are here, along with disaster victims, the displaced, and refugees seeking asylum. Good Samaritans are plentiful, along with charitable organizations that help the needy with no strings attached. Pisces is the sign in which Venus exalts, thus many artists, actors, and performers are here, whose lives have a touch of the poet that speaks to the empathy and universality of humankind.

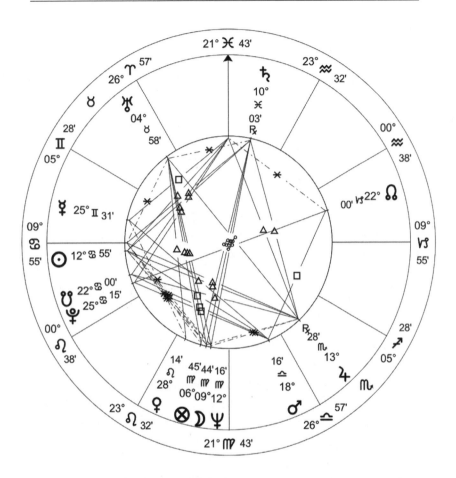

Chart 12. Pisces Midheaven: Dalai Lama XIV, July 6, 1935, 4:38 AM LMT (-6:45), Takster Village, Tibet, 36N02, 101E12.

Pisces on the Midheaven is shown in Chart 12, the 14th Dalai Lama. An internationally renowned statesman and spiritiual icon, he is also the best-selling author of *Freedom in Exile, The Art of Happiness,* and *The Art of Happiness at Work.* He was born Lhamo Thondup, the fifth of seven children, to a Tibetan barley farmer and a homemaker.

Supreme spiritual ruler of the Tibetan people, the Dalai Lama is believed by millions to be the reincarnated Buddha, also known as the Ocean of Wisdom, Holder of the White Lotus, and Kundun. Upon the death of the Dalai Lama, his monks institute a search for the Lama's reincarnation, typically a small child. Familiarity with the possessions of the previous Dalai Lama is considered the main sign of the reincarnation, and the search usually takes a few years.

In 1937, following the death of the 13th Dalai Lama in 1933, a traveling search party of monks disguised as servants selected his father's farm through a series of omens and asked to spend the night.

At that time, Lhamo Thondup was only two years old. While one of the monks played with him, the boy recognized that the monk was wearing a rosary belonging to the 13th Dalai Lama, and the little boy demanded that it be given to him. The monk agreed, but only if the boy could identify him. Young Llamo called out, "*Sera aga, Sera aga.*" *Sera* was another name for the Kwetsang Rinpochesi's monastery and *aga* is the Tibetan word for teacher or mentor. Returning in full garb several days later, the monks brought with them other possessions belonging to the 13th Dalai Lama, together with items that did not. The toddler correctly identified each object, thus convincing the monks that they had found the 14th incarnation of the Dalai Lama. The child was then installed in the thousand-room palace in Lhasa, the holy city and capital of Tibet. With a proxy ruling in his place until the child was mature and educated enough to assume his position, His Holiness received a thorough and rigorous education in logic, Tibetan art and culture, Sanskrit, medicine, and Buddhist philosophy.

On February 22, 1950, Lhamo Thondup was officially enthroned as the spiritual leader of Tibet, taking the name Jamphel Ngawang Lobsang Yeshe Tenzin Gyatso. In the summer of that same year, an earthquake shook the Tibetan mountains and the peasants declared this an omen of foreboding. Two days later communist Chinese soldiers entered Tibet, claiming to "liberate" them from imperialism. By October, there were over 80,000 Chinese soldiers occupying Tibet. Now officially enthroned as Supreme Ruler at age 15, three years prior to schedule, His Holiness spent the next nine years negotiating various peace treaties with officials in Peking with no success. On March 10, 1959, riots in Lhasa threatened His Holiness' life. On March 16th, with a few close advisers and his immediate family members His Holiness, disguised as a soldier, slipped among the crowds and began the long journey on foot and horseback to India, where the exhausted entourage arrived on March 31 and was granted political asylum. During the following years, over 80,000 Tibetans followed His Holiness to exile in India, fleeing the ravages of the Chinese occupation.

A tireless leader for world peace, the Dalai Lama has been awarded the Albert Schweitzer Humanitarian Award, the Wallenberg Award, and the Nobel Prize for Peace.

He divides his time between living an ascetic and celibate life in a remote area of northern India and traveling throughout the world promoting peace and democracy. His devout following includes individuals from every walk of life across the globe.

Chapter Two

LOCATION IS EVERYTHING—
THE PRINCIPAL PLANET

The Principal Planet is our vehicle of transport to success. Its aspect in tight orb to the Midheaven determines how we transfer our goods from raw materials to the finished product and public visibility. It describes the market-bound journey of the fisherman's boat and the first object in our vision from the high point of our personal vista.

When the Principal Planet is a conjunction, the fish are caught close to the market, with a brief and seemingly effortless return. The catch of the day is fresh, local and readily available. When the Principal Planet is a trine, the boat traveled out to sea with the tide to find its bountiful catch and the tide will ferry the boat to shore despite the distance with minimal effort on the part of the fisherman. Motors and oars are often not necessary to facilitate a smooth arrival at the market. If the Principal Planet is square the Midheaven, the boat did not need to travel as far but the tide is against the fisherman on his return trip, and the motor on the boat had to work at full capacity to bring the catch in. When the Principal Planet is sextile the Midheaven, a

---

friend suggested an excellent fishing spot, the catch is plentiful, and for half of the return trip the tide carried the boat back to the shore. When the tide changed, the motor was used, and just as the boat was having difficulty pulling in, helping hands appeared to assure a safe arrival at the dock. When the Principal Planet is in opposition to the Midheaven, the boat had to travel a great distance to find its catch, which turned out to be less than expected, but adequate, nonetheless. On the return trip, the motor failed altogether, and the fisherman had to laboriously row the boat himself against the tide for the entire distance back to shore. Despite the obstacles, however, the strenuous effort produced excellent result at the market.

Principal Planets are determined in order of their exactness to the Midheaven within signs using Ptolemaic aspects only. It is possible to have more than one Principal Planet if two planets or more are in the same degree and both aspect the Midheaven exactly. Exactness can thus be measured in minutes, but planets tied are used simultaneously. Principal Planets that are retrograde compensate for a pre-existing condition or age discrepancies; success can come very early or very late in life.

The Principal planet has a tremendous impact on the Midheaven. If the Midheaven defines one's personal market stall in the marketplace and the aspects describe the journey, the Principal Planet describes what is carried in the market basket, ferried in the fishing boat, and showcased in the stall. It short, it describes the goods.

The Sun as Principal Planet

The Sun as Principal Planet brings the power of command to the Midheaven, with the added responsibilities, privileges—and penalties—of leadership. Creative expression is emphasized, whether through artistic endeavors, children, sports or recreational activities. Naturally assuming managerial positions with grace and integrity, this placement enjoys preferential treatment and excels at giving direction, but falls short at taking it.

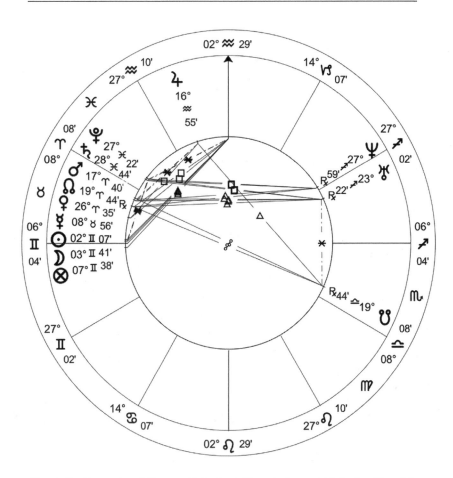

Chart 13. Example of Sun as Principal Planet: Queen Victoria, May 24, 1819, 4:15 AM LMT London, England 51N30, 0W10.

Chart 13 provides an example of the Sun as Principal Planet in the horoscope of Victoria, Queen of England.

Serving sixty-three years as the longest reigning English monarch, Victoria, fifth in succession, ascended to the throne through twists of fate and was crowned Queen of Great Britain and Ireland on June 20, 1838. Upon hearing that she was indeed to be crowned Queen, the Duke of Wellington remarked of the capable eighteen-year old woman at her first public counsel, "...Why, she not only filled the chair, she filled the room!"[1] Her very name defined an era of morality, propriety, and decorum. Victoria's reign brought England from a country of agrarian villages to the richest and most powerful nation in the world; the Sun never set on the British Empire. In keeping with her Aquarius Midheaven, Victoria presided over the rise of the Industrial Revolution, complete with the technological advancements of electricity, telephone, telegraph, typewriter, phonograph and, above all, the steam engine. This singular machine transformed the British economy and lifestyle with rail travel and steamships to reach the far-flung outposts of the Empire to facilitate sweeping social reform in England and abroad. Exceedingly willful, imperious, and terse, Victoria once wrote to an officer during the Boer War, "We are not interested in the possibilities of defeat. They do not exist." Despite her considerable reliance upon advisors such as Prime Ministers, military generals, and especially her beloved husband Prince Albert, there was no question as to who signed the document, whose word was law, who was in charge. A prolific letter writer, Victoria had musical and artistic talent and gave birth to nine children, each of whom would marry nobility to spread the dynasty and diplomacy of her empire. Her legacy thrived. At the time of her death on January 22, 1901, virtually every European king, queen, or heir presumptive was one of her grandchildren.

The Moon as Principal Planet

The Moon as Principal Planet gives a deep sense of familiarity, a need to nurture, and a shrewd and endearing sense of what the public needs to feel safe and secure. Collectors and packrats all, their boat is loaded to the gunwales with all the necessary equipment for food, clothing, and shelter. While giving the clarion call to home and hearth, they astutely respond to the ebb and flow of consumerism with their highly developed sensors. They possess excellent people skills and strive to make their market-

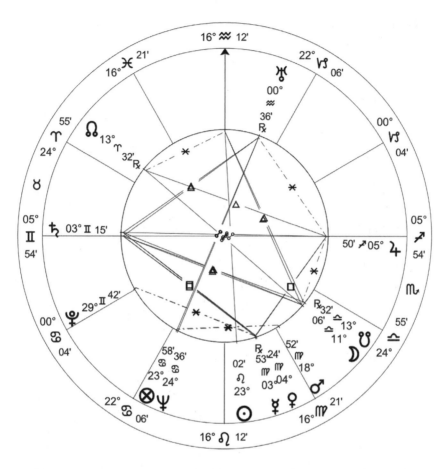

Chart 14. The Moon as Principal Planet: Julia Child, August 15, 1912, 11:30 PM PST, Pasadena, CA 34N09, 118W09.

place product a household word through their imaginative appeal to everyday people.

Chart 14, Julia Child, is an example of the Moon as Principal Planet.

American chef, author, and television personality, Julia Child is the winner of the Peabody Award for television broadcasting, an Emmy, France's Legion d'Honneur, l'Ordre National du Merité, and the first woman inducted into the Culinary Institute Hall of Fame. Long before microwaves and Martha Stewart, Child's familiar, smiling face was available in every household extolling the virtues of the table as temple. Affectionately referred to as "Our Lady of the Ladle,"[2] she "made America mad for food and changed notions of class and gender."[3]

The definitive American home cook and role model in the kitchen, Julia McWilliams was a well-to-do graduate of Smith College in 1934, who, after working in advertising for W. & J. Sloane, a furniture store in New York, joined the Office of Secret Services (OSS) when WWII broke out. Stationed in China, she met her future husband Paul Child, an artist turned OSS mapmaker. In 1948, during their first lunch in Paris, Julia Child met her fate. It happened after eating poached sole in a cream sauce served with oysters on the half shell. "I couldn't get over it. I'd never had such food in my life."[4] The die was cast, and Child was permanently hooked. After six months of training at the world-renowned cooking school Cordon Bleu, Child and two colleagues started their own school, L'Ecole des Trois Gourmandes, in Child's Left Bank apartment, giving five-dollar lessons. Ten years later, the trials and errors of these three persevering cooks in this small school produced the classic, two volume *Mastering the Art of French Cooking*, published in 1961.

During an American promotional tour for her best-selling cookbook, Child prepared an omelet on WGBH, Boston's educational television station, with her beloved husband watching in the wings. Child was a natural on camera, and her open and friendly, yet thoroughly professional manner made the producer of WGBH sit up and take notice. On February 11, 1963, 50-year-old Julia Child was featured in *The French Chef*, America's first television cooking show.

As America's most famous chef, Child cooked her way into American hearts and kitchens for over forty years. Passionate about quality, appetite, and pleasure, once during a show on baking she taste tested a brioche tart with caramel-poached fruit and a white secret sauce. When her guest chef studied her face for a reaction, Child, with tears in her eyes, was unable to speak. Finally summoning her signature voice, Child said the dessert was so good it made her cry. The show's producer explained that "she was emotionally overwhelmed by eating this thing that was so great. It tapped into something stored deep inside her."[5]

Mercury as Principal Planet

When Mercury is the Principal Planet two bilingual fishermen were in the boat to ensure continuous banter in different languages. The printed word fills the boat with memos, magazines, and books, keeping close proximity to the computers, Ipods, fax machines, and Palm Pilots that play a major role in their marketplace presentation. A flair for communications influences the life path, and frequent travel, if not an itinerant lifestyle, keeps their minds alert for the steady stream of information that will attract and absorb them. These clever wordsmiths deliver their catch and their message with elegance, efficiency, and élan.

Chart 15 on page 48 provides us with an example of Mercury as Principal Planet.

William Butler Yeats was an Irish poet, dramatist, novelist, occultist, and winner of the Nobel Prize for Literature in 1923. Hailed as one of the greatest lyric poets of the English language, Yeats published his first work, the drama *Mosada*, at age 21 after spending three years studying painting at the Metropolitan School of Art in Dublin. He was the oldest of four children of Susan Pollexfen, the scion of a well-to-do shipping family, and lawyer turned portrait artist John Yeats, whose curious blend of aesthetics and mysticism left an indelible impression on his intellectual and spiritually crusading son. The Yeats family spent their summers at the Pollexfen homestead in rural County Sligo in the West of Ireland, where the ethereal landscape and peasant culture imbued Yeats with a lifelong love of folklore. With a privileged youth and an eclectic education, Yeats evolved into a quintessential cultural creative. At age

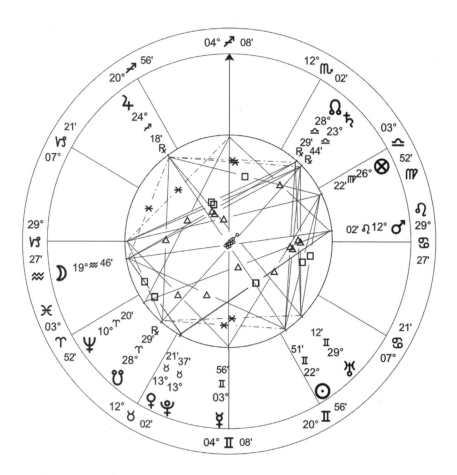

Chart 15. Mercury as Principal Planet: William Butler Yeats, June 13, 1865 10:40 PM LMT 0: 25 AM LMT + 0:25, Sandymount, Ireland, 53N58 06W2

20, he and fellow Irish poet AE (George Moore) founded the Dublin Hermetic Society. After joining the Theosophical Society of London in 1887, Yeats became a literary correspondent for two American newspapers and moved with grace in the highest artistic, literary, and political circles of his day in both London and Dublin.

Yeats' interest in ancient Irish mythology, folklore and "half forgotten things" was the theme in his first volume of poetry, *The Wanderings of Oisin and Other Poems*, published in 1889, and *Fairy and Folk Tales* in 1888. The verse drama "The Countess Cathleen" in 1892 was a unique fusion of ancient Celtic legends and contemporary Irish history. "Celtic Twilight" in 1893 caught the attention of folklorists, among them Irish dramatist Lady Augusta Gregory, who became a lifelong friend. Yeats spent twenty summers at her home Coole Park in County Galway, Ireland, a locale that served as inspiration for several major works of poetry, among them *The Secret Rose* (1897), *The Seven Woods* (1904) and *The Wild Swans at Coole* (1919). Among his best known works are "The Falling of Leaves," "The Lake Isle of Inisfree," and "When You Are Old." As the acknowledged spearhead of the Irish Literary Renaissance in the early 1900s, Yeats, together with Lady Gregory, Maude Gonne, AE, and Douglas Hyde, established the National Theatre Society, which evolved into The Abbey Theatre Company in 1904, where Yeats directed many of his own works on stage.

In 1889 Yeats' political connections brought a fated introduction to Irish revolutionary Maude Gonne, who became the single greatest influence in his life and poetry. His first and deepest love, the fiercely independent Gonne admired Yeats' poetry but continually rejected his proposals of marriage. Despite two children born out of wedlock with her French lover and her much-maligned marriage, Yeats pursued her for twenty-nine years.

An avid student of magic and astrology Yeats frequented séances and was a member of the Hermetic Order of the Golden Dawn. He was elected to the Irish Senate in 1922 and continued to write incessantly, producing works replete with symbol, image, and bardic tidings until he died in Roquebrune, France, on January 28, 1939. Upon his death, his horoscope was found among his personal papers.

> Once out of nature I shall never take
> My bodily form from any natural thing,
> But such a form as Grecian goldsmith make

Of hammered gold and gold enameling
To keep a drowsy emperor awake;
Or set upon a golden bough to sing
To lords and ladies of Byzantium
Of what is past, or passing, or to come.[6]

Venus as Principal Planet

The Venus boat is filled with paintings, sculpture, artists, crafters, singers, performers, and musical instruments of every stripe. Musicians are always on board this stunningly beautiful boat, serenading both fisherman and fish with music running the gamut from folk songs to symphonies. The fishermen look like fashion models and serve as the marketplace diplomats; they instinctively know that good manners are a survival tactic. They're shrewd bargainers, too, and demand excellence that appeals to all five senses. They achieve a delicate balance through fine-tuning the social and sensory world around them. Simply put, they wrest beauty from the deep and deliver it with style.

Chart 16 shows us an example of Venus as Principal Planet.

Billy Joel is a well-known American musician and songwriter, winner of six Grammy awards, a Tony award and inducted into the Songwriters Hall of Fame in 1992. Born William Martin Joel to two classically trained pianists, Joel was raised in Levittown, Long Island where he and his sister were raised in a musical, if not volatile, household. Coerced into piano lessons, Joel quit at age 11 due to his refusal to practice. After his parents divorced in 1957, his father returned to his native Germany and Joel would not see him again until 1973. In junior high school Joel took up the piano again as a way to meet girls and began playing professionally at night to supplement his mother's marginal income. By age 16 he was playing sessions for several recordings, including "Shangri-La" and "The Leader of the Pack." Joel's own band, The Echoes, soon had steady night gigs that became all consuming. Musical commitments outweighed

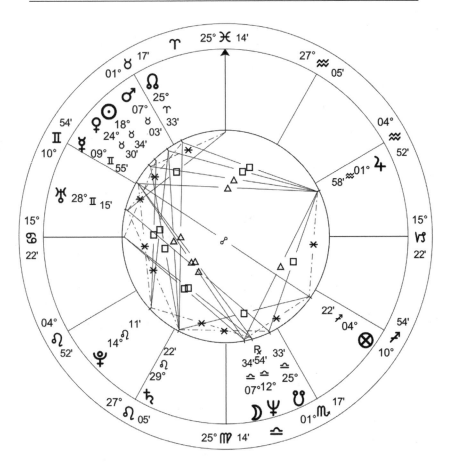

Chart 16. Venus as Principal Planet: Billy Joel, May 9 1949, 9:30 AM Bronx, NY 40N51, 73W54

his academic interests and he dropped out of high school a few months prior to graduation.

After three albums and four singles that failed commercially, Joel released his first solo album *Cold Spring Harbor* in 1971, followed by a successful promotional tour. The album drew critical acclaim but Joel, who had transformed himself from a street tough piano player into a sensitive singer/songwriter, was still dissatisfied with his career. Moving to Los Angeles one year later, Joel found his niche playing lounge piano at The Executive Room, the infamous locale that served as inspiration for his signature tune "Piano Man." His album of the same name in 1974 catapulted him to success with "Piano Man" becoming his first top-20 single and his first gold album. The following year he recorded *Streetlife Serenade*, which earned him the Cashbox award for Best New Male Vocalist. His extensive touring from his first two albums gave him recognition as a live concert attraction, culminating in sold-out performances. Now a top-billed musician and songwriter, Joel's creative output was staggering. Returning to New York in 1976, Joel released the album *The Stranger* in 1977, which captured two Grammys, followed by *52nd Street* in 1978, which hit number 1 on the charts. *Glass House* in 1980 reached number 1 for six weeks with "It's Still Rock and Roll To Me," his first number 1 single. Albums *Songs In The Attic*, 1981, *Nylon Curtain,* 1982, *An Innocent Man*, 1983, *The Bridge*, 1985, *Storm Front*, 1989, and *River of Dreams* in 1993 ranked Joel with record-breaking success, earning him the Grammy Legend Award in 1990.

In 1996 Joel hit the college lecture circuit and launched a new career designing power boats, which he sells from his The Long Island Boat Company in Montauk, New York. The Broadway show *Movin' Out,* based on twenty-six of Joel's rock ballads, won two Tony awards in 2003. In his repertoire of songs, he has no favorite. "With everything I ever wrote, I went through a pregnancy, a labor and a postpartum depression. Some of them grew up to be doctors and lawyers, and others grew up to be drug addicts and dropouts. But I love them all for different reasons."[7]

Mars as Principal Planet

This bright red fishing vessel is a speedboat, laden with every tool of the trade. The fishermen are brawny alphamales who, having little or no patience, rely heavily on sonar to find their catch long before the other boats arrive. Outfishing their peers with military efficiency and precision, they fearlessly venture into treacherous waters to haul in sharks, stingrays, and other sea creatures that are definitely not for the squeamish. Other boats keep a healthy distance from this warrior crew, for they're not keen on compromising and do not back down from a fight. Working double duty as the Coast Guard, they're the first to aid any of their fellow fishermen in an emergency, and take no heed of storm warnings.

The horoscope of Curtis Sliwa, Chart 17 on page 54, provides an example of Mars as Principal Planet.

American activist, author, and radio personality, Curtis Sliwa is the founder of The Guardian Angels, a non-profit, volunteer crime-fighting organization with forty chapters throughout the United States and seven countries worldwide. Identifiable by their red beret, this task force of crime-fighting crusaders patrols inner city neighborhoods and subways keeping law and order with martial arts, walkie-talkies, and no weapons. President's Nixon, Reagan, and Clinton, New York Mayors Rudy Giuliani, Michael Bloomberg, and numerous leaders have recognized Sliwa across the nation and the world as a leading citizen whose example of civic contribution has rarely been matched. The son of a merchant marine and a humanitarian mother, Sliwa was taught from his earliest years that helping people in need is never contingent upon gender, color, or accent, and that citizens deserve to live in safety with self-esteem, pride, and civic responsibility. A community activist since childhood, Sliwa rescued six people from a burning building in his early teens, and later created one of the nation's first recycling centers in his parent's basement, donating the proceeds to a local children's group. His standard pose of military stance with arms crossed and a stern expression belies the Good Samaritan beneath, for this "tough guy" hides a very tender heart.

As night manager in McDonald's in the South Bronx in his early twenties, Sliwa formed "The Rock Brigade," a group that conducted neighborhood clean-ups of planting and cleaning vacant lots and boarding up bombed-out buildings. Their

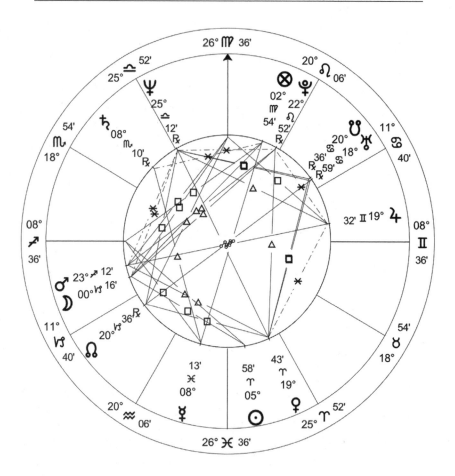

Chart 17. Example of Mars as Principal Planet: Curtis Sliwa, March 26, 1954, 11:27 PM EST Brooklyn, NY 40N38, 73W56

efforts received awards from community and municipal groups throughout the city, yet street crime was rampant. The elderly gathered in McDonald's knowing Sliwa and his coworkers would walk them safely home. Soon the "Rock Brigade" evolved into "The Mugger's Express," patrolling the subways to ensure safety. Further recruiting a multiracial team of McDonald's co-workers, Sliwa led a team of twelve crime-fighting volunteers, now known as "The Magnificent Thirteen." Riding the subways in the roughest areas and using no weapons, they isolated gang members mugging straphangers and detained them for police arrest. Volunteers soon joined their ranks and the group was officially founded on February 13, 1979. By 1982 Sliwa published StreetSmart: *The Guardian Angels Guide to Safe Living* and within a few years the number of red-bereted crusaders skyrocketed into the thousands.

Despite the highest accolades from local citizens and a fundamental need for this singular watch group, the Guardian Angles have been the subject of much controversy. Many Angels are former gang members, inciting a vicious cycle of suspicious police and gang revenge. Black belt Sliwa has been attacked with a baseball bat and shot five times due to his outspoken criticisms of members of organized crime. "I think they assumed that at that point I would put window shades on my eyes, cotton balls in my ears and a zipper on my mouth and ...shut up. I didn't. I just ratcheted it up."[8]

The charismatic and fearless Sliwa spearheads an endless array of public service programs, ranging from food and clothing distribution to administrating anti-drug speakers on the lecture circuit. Transcending the traditional territory of subways, Angels are now found in suburban settings, classrooms, and boardrooms. In 1994 Sliwa founded Cyberangels, a safety and educational program on the Internet, where specialized sentinels in virtual red berets patrol the dark alleys of cyberspace.

Jupiter as Principal Planet

This oversized boat covers the most distance of the fishing fleet, and is always seeking reasons to expand the international boundary line. These freewheeling fishermen are bon vivant, globetrotting intellectuals who seek the adventures of ocean travel while matriculating towards another academic degree. Some have worked as clergy, entertainers, jockeys, educators, booksellers, veterinarians, scientists, lawyers, athletes and pilots. Fishing takes a back seat to discussion, for this crew is continually engaged in social and philosophical debate. Frequently crossing borders to explore foreign waters, they wander into parts unknown, returning to market at their leisure with rare deepsea exotica and vast, groundbreaking knowledge. Their catch is a mere technicality when compared with their breathtaking discoveries, and brushes with authority stimulate their confrontational streak.

Chart 18 shows an example of Jupiter as Principal Planet in the horoscope of Galileo Galilei.

Italian astronomer, mathematician, inventor, physicist, teacher, and author, Galileo is considered to be the father of modern experimental science. Galileo was the oldest child of Vincenzio Galilei and Giulia Ammannati. The multi-faceted Vincenzio was a merchant, accomplished lute player, and music teacher, who conducted experiments of physical motion on lute strings to devise a new system of harmonics. Noting Galileo's unusual scientific ability, Vincenzio decided on the career of physician for his son, and sent him to study medicine, a subject in which Galileo held no interest, at the University of Pisa. Focusing on Euclid's *Elements* instead, Galileo's prodigious mathematical ability showed immediately and he quickly relinquished medicine for full-time study of physics.

By 1585 he had mastered all the extant works of Euclid and Archimedes and was teaching mathematics at Siena by public appointment. It was here that Galileo first showed himself a contentious polemic, lampooning his opponents with stinging sarcasm: "I do not feel obliged to believe that the same God who endowed us with sense, reason, and intellect intended us to forgo their use." Criticizing the custom of wearing of academic gowns, he relented to the wearing of ordinary clothes only after stating that it was best to go naked. Throughout his life he was regarded as a brilliant, charismatic genius, whose speech and pen were blistering with slander and invective. By 1589 he earned the appointment of Chair of Mathematics at the University of Pisa.

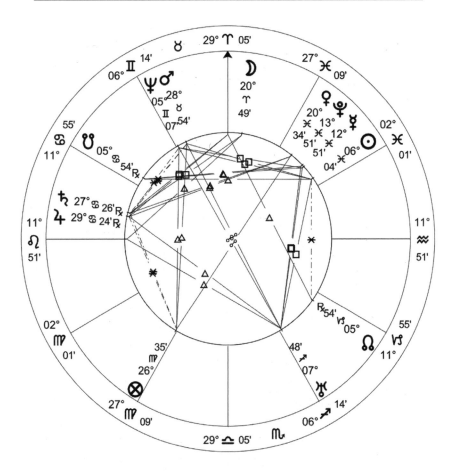

Chart 18. Jupiter as Principal Planet: Galileo Galilei, February 15, 1564, OS 3:31 PM LMT, Pisa, Italy 43N43, 10E23

While climbing the winding staircase in the city's Leaning Tower, he allegedly dropped two weights—a large cannonball and a small musketball—and proved that they fell at the same rate of speed, instantly disproving Aristotle's theory that an object's rate of descent is proportional to its weight. He further disproved Aristotle by determining that falling objects do not move with constant speed but accelerate in motion. Pondering a ceiling lamp in the cathedral at Pisa, he noticed the constant regularity of its swing, and wondered how its speed was determined. Rigorous experimentation resulted in the pendulum theory. These milestones of discovery resulted in Galileo's continuous application of mathematics to nature. Not only did the 25-year-old math teacher disprove the universally accepted ancient laws of physics and discover new theories of his own; he proved all of them through experiment with irrefutable evidence. Further mathematical application produced his invention of the proportional compass for precise measurement.

Securing a post at the University of Padua that tripled his previous salary, Galileo taught medical students Euclid's geometry and astronomy in order to utilize astrology in their medical practice. In 1610 he began experimenting with the doctrine of refraction to improve the recent phenomenon of the spyglass. Grinding and polishing his own lenses, he designed a telescope that could magnify thirty times. Naming it *perspicillum*, he turned it toward the night sky, where he observed mountains on the Moon, four bodies surrounding Jupiter, the multitude of tiny stars that comprised the Milky Way, and sunspots. His subsequent reports on the rings of Saturn and the phases of Venus led him to his theory that Venus must orbit the Sun, not the Earth. In 1616 he was formally censured and forbidden to publish theories that supported the Copernican model of the universe. Despite this warning, continuous publications supporting the blasphemous Copernican theory that the Earth and all other planets rotated around the Sun culminated in a Papal Inquisition in 1633, where Galileo was threatened with punishment by torture if he did not rescind his heretical statements. Exasperated and in poor health, he retracted his statement, but was still found guilty of heresy for publishing heretical theories. A verdict of lifelong imprisonment was commuted to house arrest and, blinded by cataracts, he spent his final years in his home under close watch of officers of the Inquisition.

Saturn as the Principal Planet

This is the model fishing boat against which all other vessels are judged. Its no-nonsense design invokes a conservative image, yet its classic construction permits it to withstand extreme weather conditions. Its anchor is a prominent, foreboding feature to secure its place to the ocean floor below, for shifting of position is not tolerated. The well-mannered, uniformed fishermen work double shifts to ensure their reputations of maintaining the time-honored tradition of procuring the best quality fish for a discriminating clientele. This disciplined, high-achieving crew is capable, shrewd, and ambitious, with an aura of sophistication. Mindful of fishing within strict boundaries, they strive to move up the ranks in the chain of command and leave no stone unturned to please their master and commander. Shakespeare captured them perfectly in the phrase, "Mine honor is my life, both grow in one. Take honor from me, and my life is done."

Saturn as Principal Planet is shown in Chart 19 on page 60, the horoscope of Elizabeth II, Queen of England.

Queen of England and Head of the Commonwealth of the United Kingdom, Elizabeth Alexandra Mary Windsor is the first child of the Duke and Duchess of York, who later became King George VI and Queen Elizabeth. From the age of two, the young Elizabeth was trained in the proper etiquette as a member of the Royal Family, displaying impeccable manners with an inbred sense of duty and responsibility of what was expected of her as a future monarch. Raised in a close, protected environment, she and her younger sister Margaret were educated at home during her early years by their mother, tutors, and governesses. At age ten she became Princess Elizabeth upon her father's succession to the throne and was declared heir presumptive. She began studying constitutional history and law at this time, along with music, art, and theatre. Displaying a strong interest in sports, dogs, and country life, she was a keen equestrian from her early youth.

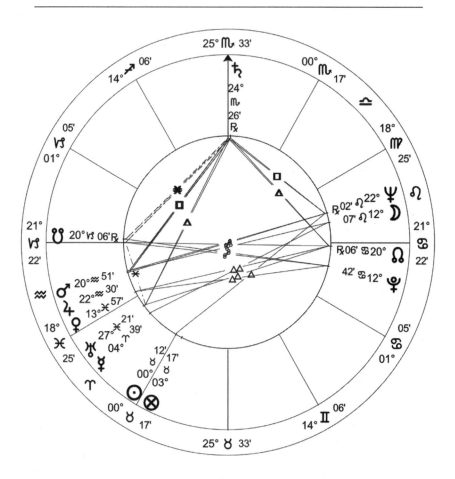

Chart 19. Saturn as Principle Planet: Queen Elizabeth II. April 21, 1926, 2:40 AM GMT London, England. 51N30, 0W00.

Princess Elizabeth began to actively participate in public life at age 14, when she broadcast a radio message on the BBC to the children of Britain and the Commonwealth who were being evacuated for safety during WWII. At 16 she made her first public engagement when inspecting the regiment, and the following year made her first solo public engagement while spending a day with a tank battalion in the Southern Command. Other engagements soon followed in 1944 as Counselor of State on a tour of

Italian battlefields, where she carried out duties as Head of State. Contributing to the War Effort, she knitted socks and scarves for the soldiers, and in early 1945 trained as an auto mechanic and ambulance driver, reaching the rank of Junior Commander by the end of the war. "It's all to do with the training," she once said. "You can do a lot if you're properly trained."

On November 20, 1947 Princess Elizabeth married her fourth cousin, Navy Lieutenant Philip Mountbatten, whom she had known since her early teens. Upon his marriage to Elizabeth he became His Royal Highness Prince Philip, Duke of Edinburgh. Their first child, Prince Charles, was born on November 14, 1948, followed by Princess Anne on August 15, 1950. Leaving her royal children to be raised by governesses in London, Princess Elizabeth and Prince Philip spent the next three years traveling to France, Greece, and Canada and living abroad in Malta. In January 1952 Princess Elizabeth's father, George VI, was scheduled in Australia and New Zealand on royal duties. When illness prevented him from traveling, Elizabeth took his place. On February 6, during the first leg of her trip in Kenya, Africa, she received word of her father's untimely death of a heart attack in his sleep and her resultant accession to the throne.

Her coronation was held at Westminster Abbey on June 2, 1953. It was the first coronation to be broadcast on television, bringing ancient regal splendor into homes around the world. Two sons followed, Prince Andrew on February 19, 1960 and Prince Edward, on March 10, 1964, respectively. During her reign, the Queen has witnessed fundamental changes to her sceptered isle, with nationalized industries, mass immigration, and independence granted to over forty former British colonies and territories. One of the wealthiest women in the world, she agreed in 1992 to having her phenomenal income taxed for the first time in history. While the Sun now sets on her British empire, it seldom sets on the scandals, infidelities, and shenanigans of her royal family.

The Outer Planets

When the Outer Planets function as Principal Planets, the individual rarely settles for a mainstream career. They take the road less traveled and then wander off the beaten path to hear the different drummer, who beckons them to embrace a career independent of clocks, ledger sheets, tax returns, and other trappings of mundane life. Working routine jobs in their youth enabled them to fine-tune the skills they needed to survive, however they develop themselves not to move up the proverbial ladder of success, but to rather jump off it and erect another ladder of their own definition. The more that outer planets serve as the Principal Planet the more the individual is inclined to create their own niche and not follow the herd into a day job, or at least not remain in it for longer than necessary. The personal planet in closest orb to the Midheaven after the Principal Planet usually determines the career path taken prior to hearing the different drummer, an event that is often triggered by transits and progressions. Once the drumbeat evolves into a rhythm, they're following their own rocky road to bliss. And the beat goes on.

Uranus as Principal Planet

This fishing boat is unlike any other boat in the fleet. More a floating science project than a fishing vessel, it is equipped with state of the art computers, modems, satellite dishes, and wide screen monitors to make fishing a virtual experience. Such technological advances streamline the workload to leave time for this fishing crew of highly intelligent techies to define visionary goals and establish a New World Order. Humanists all, they embrace egalitarianism and promote freedom in all its forms, for there is no rank and file here; all work together to foster communal well-being. They fish where and when they please because as far as they're concerned, the ocean is not private property. If discord with authority arises, beware the rising flag of skull and crossbones. Mutiny may rise with the tide.

An example of Uranus as Principal Planet is the horoscope of Che Guevara, Chart 20 on page 64.

Argentine revolutionary, doctor, and author, Ernesto Guevara de la Sena was the oldest of five children born to a moderately leftist engineer and his intellectual wife. Severely asthmatic from age two, Guevara was home-schooled in youth by his mother, and then educated himself in his father's extensive library until 1941 when he began attending secondary school in Cordoba. Enrolling in the University of Buenos Aires in 1948, he pursued a career in medicine, specializing in dermatology. Disqualified for military service due to asthma, he traveled extensively throughout northern Argentina in his late teens, studying tropical diseases among small villages and indigenous tribes. Shocked at the poverty of his fellow countrymen he was determined to see more of how the other half lived, and in 1951 Guevara and his friend Alberto Granado traveled on motorcycles down coastal Argentina into Chile, Peru, Colombia, and Venezuela, where they worked in a leper colony. His diary from this adventure was later published as *The Motorcycle Diaries: A Journey Around South America* and made into a film in 2004.

In 1952 Guevara joined in the riotous protest against Argentine dictator Juan Peron.

Earning his degree the following year, Guevara practiced medicine in Guatemala, joining the pro-Communist regime of President Jacobo Arbenz Guzman. Central America and the United States, whose Guatemalan interests included the United Fruit Company, overthrew Arbenz in 1953. Guevara, noting the role the CIA played in the counterrevolution, organized a resistance. Ultimately faced with defeat, he escaped to Mexico City in 1954 where he befriended fellow political refugee Fidel Castro and immersed himself in the invasion of Cuba.

Under Castro's influence, Guevara studied Mao Tse Tung and wrote his first book, *Guerilla Warfare,* in 1961. During this

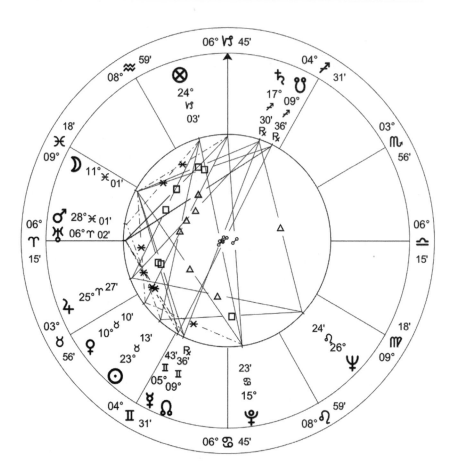

Chart 20. Uranus as Principal Planet: Che Guevara, May 14, 1928 3:05 AM AST Rosaria, Argentina. 32S57, 60W40.

time he began addressing everyone as Che, an Argentine expression for friend or comrade, and thus a legend was born.

In 1956, Castro, Che, and their Communist insurgents landed in Cuba, initiating a rebel invasion and three-year guerilla war against dictator Fulgencio Batista. Originally included in the expedition for his medical expertise, Che quickly rose to become Commandant of the Revolutionary Army of Barbutos, a title that made him directly responsible for the executions of dozens of defectors and Batista loyalists. By 1959 he was granted Cuban citizenship and was second only to Castro, who appointed him Governor of the National Bank. After the fall of Batista in January 1959, Che served as Minister of Industry from 1961–1965. Increasingly hostile towards American interest in the Cuban economy, he redirected Cuba's traditional sugar export from America to the Communist bloc and advocated nuclear confrontation during the Cuban Missile Crisis.

Finding his true calling to be a charismatic revolutionary rather than healer or politician, Che formally rejected Soviet Communism in a speech delivered on February 1965, calling instead for increased guerilla warfare in South America, Asia, and Africa. With their revolutionary ideals now polarized, Castro removed Che from office and severed all ties. Going underground that same year, Che led a group of Cubans to fight in the Kinshasa rebellion in the Congo. Withdrawing from this failed effort several months later, he discarded his famous beret, shaved his head, and disguised himself as an Uruguayan economist to travel through Latin America incognito.

In November 1966 he surfaced in Bolivia leading a band of peasant guerillas to inspire a revolution that would "trigger twenty Vietnams." A Bolivian battalion cornered the ragged militia, capturing Che on October 8, 1967. Refusing all attempts at interrogation by CIA and Bolivian officials, he was executed by firing squad the following day.

His book *Man and Socialism in Cuba* was published that same year followed by *Reminiscences of the Cuban Revolutionary War* in 1968.

Neptune as Principal Planet

Often shrouded by an inexplicable fog, this boat has the appearance of a ghost ship. Surrounded by ethereal music and strange lights, it is draped in nets that camouflage its nondescript structure. Lacking navigational equipment, it sails with the tide to no predetermined destination, guided only by high-frequency sensors. Granting sanctuary to all on board, it houses a steam room, cinema, cocktail lounge, rehab and spiritual retreat center, hospital, and hospice. The fishermen, as fine-tuned as their vessel, are saints, artists, bon vivants, and outcasts, who either soar in the ether waves of divine creativity or dredge the ocean floor for lost souls. On intimate terms with the peaks and valleys of the human condition, these selfless, compassionate anglers fish in the Twilight Zone. Dolphins lead them back to port, where they donate their catch to charity.

Chart 21, the horoscope of Raoul Wallenberg, presents an example of Neptune as Principal Planet.

Wallenberg was a Swedish architect, businessman, diplomat, and humanitarian who helped rescue over 100,000 Hungarian Jews during World War II. Born to one of Sweden's most distinguished families, Wallenberg's father, a naval officer, died of cancer three months before his son's birth. Gustav Wallenberg, his paternal grandfather, supervised his grandson's education with the plan for him to continue the family tradition in banking, but the youth's interests were in architecture and business. After graduating secondary school in 1930, with top honors in Russian and drawing, Wallenberg moved to the USA the following year to study architecture at the University of Michigan. Graduating with highest honors in 1935, he returned to Sweden and found little or no career prospects. Grandfather Gustav helped him get a job selling building materials with a Swedish company in Cape Town, South Africa, then placed him at a Dutch bank in Haifa, Palestine, six months later. In Palestine, Wallenberg met Jews who had escaped the Holocaust and was deeply affected by their stories of Nazi persecution. Perhaps Wallenberg felt a distant bond; his great-great-grandfather was a Jew.

Wallenberg finally settled in a job with a Swedish exporting company in Budapest. Thanks to the freedom of movement of his Swedish passport and his excellent job performance, the multilingual Wallenberg was promoted to Director of International Relations eight months later. His business trips through

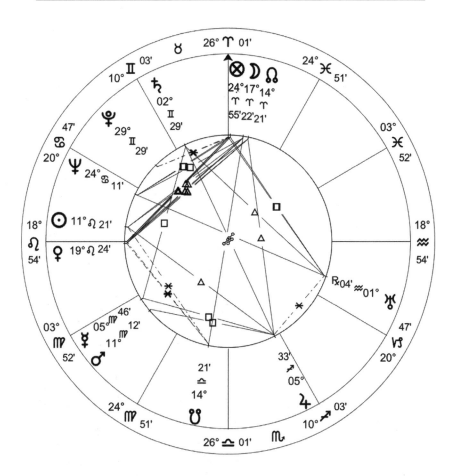

Chart 21. Neptune as Principal Planet: Raoul Wallenberg, August 4, 1912, 4:35 AM, MET, Stockholm, Sweden, 59N20, 18E03.

Nazi-occupied France and Germany brought further testimony of Jewish persecution. In 1944 President Roosevelt established the War Refugee Board, which worked with Jewish organizations, diplomats, and resistance groups throughout Europe to rescue Jews from occupied territory. Under this cover, Roosevelt appointed Wallenberg as first secretary to the Swedish legation in Budapest. His task was to reroute as many of the 230,000 Jews remaining in the city from Adolf Eichmann's notorious transports. Wallenberg supervised the creation and distribution of thousands of neutral Swedish passports along with setting up nurseries, hospitals and soup kitchens. Hanging signs that read "Swedish Library" and "Swedish Research Institute" on Red Cross buildings, and hanging the Swedish flag on "Swedish Houses" on thirty locations throughout the city, he established hiding places for some 15,000 displaced Jews. When Eichmann began marching Jews out of Budapest on November 20, 1944, Wallenberg ran along the rows handing out forged Swedish protective passes, food and medicine. Threatening and bribing the Gestapo, he was able to have all Jews holding protective passes released from the march. Discovering one of Eichmann's trains full of Jews, Wallenberg climbed to the top of the rail cars, ran long the roofs, and stuffed protective passes through windows. Nazi soldiers opened fire on him, but were so impressed with his courage they deliberately aimed too high. Jumping to the ground unharmed, Wallenberg demanded that all those holding protective passes be released from the train and follow him. Permission was granted.

Wallenberg's greatest coup was in January 1945, when he learned that Eichmann planned a total massacre of the Budapest ghetto. Wallenberg had an ally deliver a note to the Commander-in-Chief of the German troops in Hungary, informing him that he would be held personally responsible for the massacre and that he would be hanged as a war criminal. The massacre was stopped immediately. Two days later, Russian soldiers arrived to find 97,000 Jews alive in the Budapest ghetto.

Wallenberg was speaking to a Russian soldier in front of a Swedish House on January 13, 1945, requesting, and receiving, permission to visit the Soviet military headquarters in the city of Drebcen, east of Budapest. Four days later he departed to Drebcen under Russian escort. He was never seen again.

Pluto as Principal Planet

Resembling a stealth vehicle more than a fishing boat, this vessel can metamorphose, running the gamut from submarine, to brothel, to floating Emergency Room, to research center. There's a Danger, Keep Out sign prominently displayed along with an invisible, electric fence surrounding their slip in the harbor. It probes the ocean floor for bottom-feeders, sunken ships, buried treasure, and lost civilizations. Piranhas, blowfish, and other poisonous denizens of the deep are no strangers to this leather-clad crew, who appear both sexual and dangerous. This aquatic S.W.A.T. team can transform their appearance before your very eyes into pirates, potentates, detectives, sexual predators, surgeons, shamans, and psychiatrists. They know what lurks. They take no prisoners. But they'll earn your respect.

The horoscope of Amy Fisher presents an example of Pluto as Principal Planet, shown as Chart 22 on page 70. Amy Fisher is infamous as the American teenager known as "The Long Island Lolita," who was active in the sex trade and became a media sensation for the attempted murder of her lover's wife.

Amy was born in 1974, the only child of prodigiously over-indulgent parents who gave her everything but discipline and guidance. Deeply troubled in youth, she ran away from home at age 11, and again on February 24, 1991, at the age of 16.

Her over-the-top rebellious behavior and underachieving performance in school led her parents to seek professional help for their daughter, who claimed at age 13 that a workman in their home sexually molested her. In July 1991, at age 16, she began an affair with Joey Buttafuoco, a married auto mechanic twenty years her senior, shortly after she had taken her car to his auto shop for repairs. In August 1991, when Fisher needed money, Joey allegedly set her up to work with an escort agency, and the torrid affair continued while Fisher was apparently working as a prostitute. On May 19, 1992, Amy went to his home and shot his wife, Mary Jo Buttafuoco, in the face with a pistol on her doorstep, leaving her partially paralyzed. Pleading guilty to

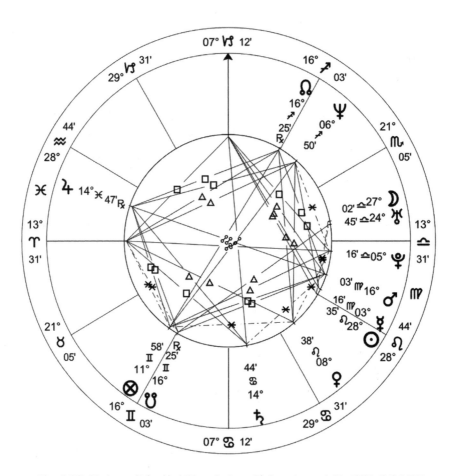

Chart 22. Pluto as Principal Planet: Amy Fisher, August 21, 1974, 9:26 PM EDT, Oceanside, NY 40N38, 73W38.

assault charges on September 22, 1992, Amy, who had claimed that the gun went off accidentally, was sentenced to prison, where she earned her high school equivalency. Seven years later, Mary Jo Buttafuoco, with a .25 caliber bullet still lodged in her neck, informed the New York State parole board that she had forgiven Amy, who was released that same year. Joey Buttafuoco served four months for statutory rape. He then moved to California and pursued a career in B movies and celebrity boxing.

The trial of the debauched duo became a nation-wide obsession that inspired comic books, trading cards, three television movies, and a musical. After her release from prison, Amy made every attempt to turn her life around. She struggled from job to job, her employment usually being thwarted whenever a boss or coworker recognized her. Determined to shed her past, she dodged the press, changed her name, had cosmetic surgery and earned a college degree in business management. When dating while on parole proved prohibitive, she switched to Match.com, where she met her husband, Lou, twenty-five years her senior, a retired cop turned wedding photographer. After the birth of her son in 2001, the former "Long Island Lolita" began writing an advice column for incarcerated women in the *Long Island Press* in 2002, using it as a campaign to end the abuse of women in prison. In 2004, Amy penned the New York Times bestseller, *If I Knew Then*, detailing her lurid affair, the shooting, her prison years, lessons learned, and the redemption of her life. In October 2004, she began a career as a radio anchor on a drive-time show "The Morning Brew" on WBON-FM, Ronkonkoma, NY. Her daughter was born in 2005.

By October 2007 Amy and her husband Bellera were estranged, and Amy Fisher was again in the news: the *New York Post* published allegations that Fisher's husband sold a sex tape of the couple to a video company in Los Angeles. Amy is now fighting to suppress its release.

Chapter 3

DIGNITIES, MUTUAL RECEPTIONS, AND
MAJOR CONFIGURATIONS

*We understand complex things by systematically breaking
them into successively simpler parts and understanding
how these parts fit together locally.*

DONALD E. KNUTH[1]

Dignities

Planets, like people, like to feel comfortable. They function in
the twelve signs of the horoscope that serve as styles in which
the energies of the planets are expressed.

Planets in Dignity

When a planet is in dignity, it is at home in its own sign. The
planet is dressed in comfortable clothes and is safe and secure
in its own home. It relaxes in a serene environment throughout
the life of the individual. It enjoys favor and contentment and is
protected from harm. It's a type of planetary pedigree.

Planets in Exaltation

Planets in exaltation enjoy high status and operate in a sphere of entitlement. Always dressed in high fashion, they appear to be carried along on a wave of honor and privilege, living in luxury and manifesting the energies of the planet. High living has its price, however, and exaltation does not guarantee a lifetime of benefit. When one is on the top, the only place to go is down. Exalted planets are not protected from the glare of the spotlight and intruding paparazzi. As points of overriding concern, the exaggerated energies of these planets produce extreme highs and lows with little equilibrium. Any house or houses ruled by exalted planets are areas that take front-and-center focus.

Planets in Detriment

Planets in detriment are planets in signs opposite to their own sign and thus their own nature. They are dressed in borrowed, poorly fitted clothing and are living in someone else's home where they are unfamiliar with and unsuited to their surroundings. Like strangers in a strange land, they struggle to survive with basic amenities and function at a disadvantage.

Planets in Fall

Planets in fall are planets in signs opposite to their sign of exaltation. To be the opposite of exalted means to be held in low status. Thus planets in signs of fall are weakened, homeless, and in poor health. They are not only in alien territory, they cannot speak the lingua franca to communicate their needs. Planets in fall, and any houses that they rule, need assistance from aspects to other planets and angles.

Mutual Receptions

Mutual reception occurs when two planets occupy each other's signs to their benefit. For example, the Sun in Cancer and Moon in Leo, are in mutual reception, as are Mercury in Sagittarius and Jupiter in Gemini. It's as if the planets are shaking hands in a friendly, equitable manner. In the Slevin System, mutual receptions can also perform in the signs of each other's exaltation, such as Mars in Virgo and Mercury in Capricorn. The planets are shaking hands wearing dress gloves, giving the interaction status and increasing their mutual benefit. Mixed mutual reception can also occur, when two planets are in the signs of each other's exaltation and dignity, such as Jupiter in Taurus and Venus in Cancer. A mixed mutual reception is less balanced than the others; one planet in dress gloves is shaking the bare hand of the other, but they still get along despite incongruent attire. Mutual reception in detriment and fall are not used in the Slevin System, for these placements will not bring you success. Negative exchanges are seldom of benefit.

Chart 23 on page 76, Al Gore, is an example of Midheaven ruler in mutual reception.

Al Gore is an American politician, and an award-winning author and film documentarian. The 45th Vice President of the United States from 1993–2001, Al Gore brought his noted family name, impressive education, military service, and impeccable reputation to serve in the Oval Office under Bill Clinton. The only son of Senator Albert Gore, Sr. from Tennessee and law school graduate Pauline LaFon, Gore enjoyed a privileged childhood and adolescence, attending the prestigious St. Alban's school in Washington D.C. Learning how the other half lives, he spent his summers at his family farm in Carthage, Tennessee, working as a day laborer with cattle and crops. After graduating Harvard with a degree in government in 1969, he enlisted in the army in August of that same year where he trained as a military journalist. He married Mary Aitheson, "Tipper," on May 19, 1970 and, despite his opposition to the war, he felt a civic duty to serve and shipped out to Vietnam as a war correspondent in early 1971.

Returning to civilian life, he and Tipper bought a farm in Carthage, Tennessee, where Gore worked as a reporter for the *Tennessean* in Nashville and attended Vanderbilt University, his

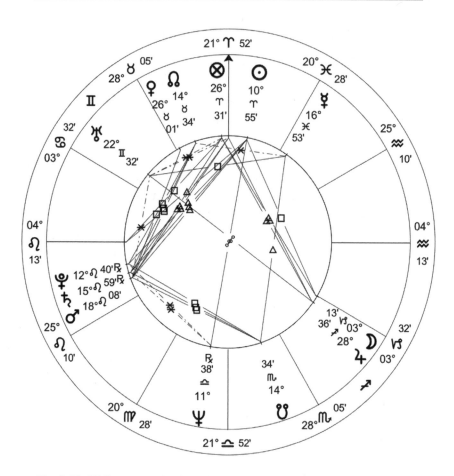

Chart 23. Midheaven ruler in Mutual Reception: Al Gore, March 31, 1948, 12:53 PM EST Washington, DC. 38N54, 77W02.

mother's alma mater. He studied divinity and law, but did not earn a degree in either discipline.

Gore ran for an open seat in Tennessee's third Congressional District in the spring of 1976 and won. He was re-elected in 1978, 1980, and 1982 and, following in his dad's footsteps, he won a seat on the Senate in 1984. Re-elected in 1990, he became the first candidate to carry virtually all ninety-five counties in Tennessee. He ran for President in 1988, winning Democratic primaries and caucuses in seven states, but lost his candidacy to Michael Dukakis of Massachusetts.

In April 1989, Gore's only son was hit by a car, suffering serious injuries. Gore and Tipper kept a continuous bedside vigil for over four months, during which time Gore began writing the book, *Earth in the Balance,* which became a bestseller. After extensive surgery and therapy, his son recovered, but the harrowing experience left Gore politically adrift, and he left public life to devote more time to his family.

After serving as Vice President under Bill Clinton for two terms, Gore made his own run for the Oval Office, announcing his campaign for the presidency on June 16, 1999. On November 7, 2000, Republican George W. Bush defeated him in the most bitterly contested election in American history, including multiple recounts and a Supreme Court decision. The final decision voted 7–2 to declare the ongoing recount procedure unconstitutional, with a 5–4 to ban further recounts using other recounting methods.

In January 2001, Gore launched a teaching career in journalism at Columbia University's graduate school, and now serves on the board of directors of Apple Computers, and is the unofficial advisor to Google's senior management. Though deeply concerned about America's future in the global age, he has publicly declared not to return to politics. His 2006 documentary on global warming, *An Inconvenient Truth,* won an Academy Award for Best Documentary Film (2007), and his efforts in the fight against global warming earned him the Nobel Prize for Peace in 2007.

Uranus serves as Gore's Principal Planet, noting independence, progressive thinking, and a desire to serve humanity. While his political career reflected these qualities, Mars, ruler of the Midheaven, is in mutual reception with the Sun, ruler of his Ascendant. Thus the rulers of his personal and public presentations are engaged in a compatible handshake, what you see is what you get. Midheaven-ruling Mars rising in the first house illustrates how he aggressively pursued a high profile public presentation from his youth. The Sun, ruler of his Ascendant, exalted in the ninth, points to his inclination toward academics, law, divinity, and publishing. These extremely fortunate angular rulers indicate high status from birth (Ascendant) due to planetary pedigree and to his highly successful career in the public eye (Midheaven).

• • •

The horoscope of Charles "Lucky" Luciano, Chart 24, provides an example of Midheaven ruler in Mixed Mutual Reception.

Lucky Luciano was a Sicilian-American gangster who created what is now known as the American Mafia. His legendary racketeering gave him a subterranean status that catapulted him into the highest echelons of international government intrigue and military operations.

Born Salvatore Lucania in a small town outside Palermo, Italy, Luciano's father worked in the sulfur mines, laboring in vain to raise his family from their abject poverty. The family emigrated to the Lower East Side of New York City in 1906, where young Lucania was arrested the following year for shoplifting. Soon after his arrest he started his first racket. For a penny a day, he would give Jewish schoolchildren protection against beatings while walking to school. After refusal of payment on one occasion Luciano attacked a particularly small, underweight child named Majer Suchowlinski, and was shocked to discover that the gritty waif gave as good as he got, despite his obvious disadvantage in size and weight. The skirmish resulted in a lifelong partnership, and the waif shortened his name to Meyer Lansky.

At 16 Luciano was convicted of peddling heroin and morphine and was committed to a reformatory for six months. By age 19 Luciano was one of the leaders of the notorious Five Points Gang and was a prime suspect in a number of murders. His notoriety increased, and four years later he was a notable bootlegger during Prohibition. Mafia chiefs took notice of the young Luciano, who admired the way the chiefs bought protection from both politicians and police.

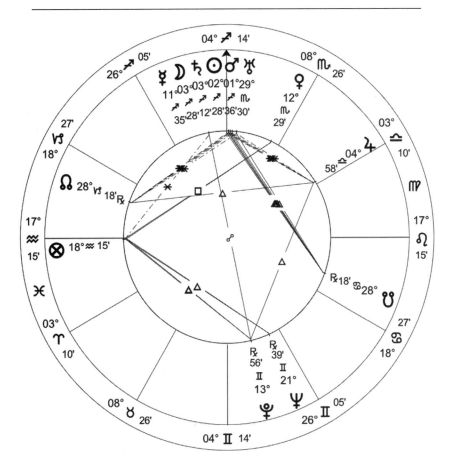

Chart 24. Midheaven Ruler in Mixed Mutual Reception: Charles "Lucky" Luciano, November 24, 1897, 12:00 PM, MET, Lercara Friddi, Sicily, 37N45 13E36

By the late 1920s Luciano was chief lieutenant in the largest Mafia family in New York, working directly under its boss, Giuseppe "Joe the Boss" Masseria. The progressive Luciano had no patience for Masseria's old-world style of refusing to do business with those of any other nationality. Luciano, believing that such insularity was an unnecessary obstacle to making a profit, secretly joined forces with underbosses of the opposing crime family of Salvatore Marranzano and plotted Masseria's demise. But the details leaked.

In October, 1929, Luciano was forced into a limousine with drawn curtains on Sixth Avenue in New York. It was to be a one-way ride. Inside the limo Luciano was savagely beaten, stabbed, and ultimately left for dead when his unconscious body was thrown from the car thirty miles away on a Staten Island beach. He miraculously regained consciousness hours later and staggered a mile to the local police station. Noting his near-death condition, he was rushed to a hospital for treatment. Detectives began questioning him, but ever-lucid Luciano remembered the code of Omerta and gave no answers, firmly telling them, "Don't you cops lose any sleep over it, I'll attend to this thing myself later."[2] Surviving a lacerated throat and permanent damage to his eye and face, Luciano, grateful for his life and now justifiably fearing for it, changed his name to Lucky. While he was aware of the infighting between the families, he initially didn't know who would want him dead. He found out who ordered his abduction: Joe the Boss Masseria. On April 15, 1930, four of Luciano's gunmen murdered Masseria in a Coney Island restaurant.

Luciano was now off and running as the archetypal gangster, setting up a national crime syndicate with Mafia chiefs in Chicago, Detroit, New Jersey and, above all, New York. By the mid 1930s he controlled almost all the brothels in New York, setting a flat rate and working the prostitutes over sixty hours a week. After police raided eighty separate brothels, prostitutes reviled the brutal regime of Luciano's crew. In 1936, Luciano received a sentence of 30–60 years for his involvement.

The mysterious loss of ships in the Hudson River during World War II led stymied Naval Intelligence to enlist the help of Luciano to secure the New York waterfront docks from possible Nazi sabotage. Luciano agreed to cooperate, on the grounds that he could conduct his "business operations" from his cell. The deal was set, with Cardinal Spellman, the Archbishop of New York serving as the intermediary between Luciano and

President Franklin Roosevelt. Luciano's control of the docks was absolute. Longshoremen, fishermen, and waterfront racketeers became the eyes and ears of U.S. Naval Intelligence. Soon eight German spies were arrested and maps and blueprints for sabotage were seized. When the Invasion of Sicily was planned, Lucianos's assistance proved inestimable. On July 9, 1943, General Patton and 160,000 Allied troops landed in Sicily. Five days later an American fighter plane flew over the village of Villalba, dropping a canvas sack addressed to "Zu Calo." Zu Calo was the nickname of Don Calogero Vizzini, the undisputed chief of the Sicilian Mafia. The sack contained a yellow scarf with a large black L, which stood, of course, for Lucky Luciano. Lucky's relatives were members of Zu Calo's crew, and together with the Sicilian Mafia they safeguarded roads from snipers and provided guides and interpreters for General Patton and his battalion for a seamless military invasion, all commanded from a prison cell in upstate New York.[3]

For his invaluable cooperation in military affairs, Luciano's sentence was commuted on the condition that he be deported to Italy. On February 10, 1946, Luciano sailed from his beloved city of New York. In Italy, Luciano returned to the narcotics trade, establishing a definitive alliance with the Corsican Mafia, who maintained their stronghold in Marseilles, France. Their drug operation was called "The French Connection," recounted in the film starring Gene Hackman. Soon heroin flooded American and European cities, fueled by the Mafia's expansion of control in the music and entertainment industry. Luciano's legacy of narcotic racketeering continued beyond his death.

Luciano died of a heart attack at age 64 on January 26, 1962 in Naples International Airport. He was on his way to meet an American movie producer to make his life story into a film. Rumor has it the Mafia poisoned him en route.

The mixed mutual reception in Luciano's chart occurs between Jupiter in Libra and Saturn in Sagittarius. Jupiter, ruler of Luciano's Midheaven, is the sign in which Saturn is exalted and Saturn is in the sign that Jupiter rules. Since Jupiter and Saturn rule Luciano's 10th, 11th and 12th, and 1st house respectively, these houses also play a role in pointing to success in Luciano's life. His career (10th) was linked to the Mafia, a group (11th) that operated from behind the scenes (12th). Luciano's physical body and appearance (1st) was permanently scarred from his career and associations, and it was these very scars that were used as identifying marks on his FBI mug shot and rap sheet. His Part of Fortune conjunct his Ascendant (first) undoubtedly helped him survive his vicious assault when he was left for dead. And it was his status and rank (10th) that success-fully enabled him to coordinate a strategic military attack from inside his prison cell (12th). See how it works?

• • •

An example of Mutual Reception by Exaltation is shown in Chart 25, John F. Kennedy.

American author, politician, and the thirty-fifth President of the United States, John F. Kennedy was the first Roman Catho-lic and the youngest man ever to be elected to the nation's high-est office. He was the second of nine children born to Joseph and Rose Fitzgerald Kennedy. Father Joe was the U.S. ambas-sador to Great Britain and Mother Rose was the daughter of "Honey Fitz," the mayor of Boston. The power of politics was the family mantra.

From his earliest years Kennedy displayed a brilliant intellect and a vast array of baffling medical symptoms. His continuous poor health often prevented him from spending a complete year in school, and he spent much time in specialized hospitals and clinics throughout America for treatment of chronic colitis and possible leukemia. His privileged childhood in the fabled Ken-nedy family gave him advantages of summers at the family com-pound in Hyannis Port, Cape Cod and Christmas at the family estate in Palm Beach, Florida. Five grammar schools and two high schools later, he graduated Choate and, after six months in Princeton, he followed in his beloved older brother Joe's foot-steps and entered Harvard, where he graduated cum laude in

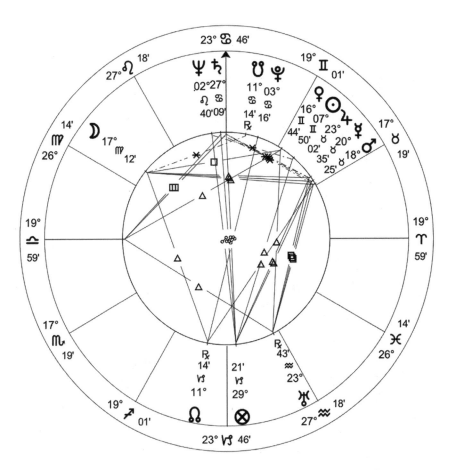

Chart 25. Mutual Reception by Exaltation: John F. Kennedy. May 29, 1917, 3:00 PM EST, Brookline, Massachusetts, 42N20, 71W07.

1940 with a degree in international affairs. His senior thesis was entitled "Appeasement in Munich." At his father's encouragement, Kennedy published his thesis as a book that same year, entitled *Why England Slept*. It became a bestseller. At age 21, Father Joe bestowed a one million-dollar trust fund to Kennedy. In 1941 Kennedy volunteered for the Navy but was rejected due to a chronic back problem that was probably created from steroid use to combat his illnesses. Father Joe's connections turned rejection into acceptance and, as an ensign, Kennedy worked directly under the Secretary to the Navy. After a tour of duty in Panama and the Pacific Theater, he was promoted to lieutenant, commanding a patrol torpedo (PT) boat.

On August 2, 1943, in the Solomon Islands, a Japanese destroyer rammed Kennedy's PT boat, causing further injury to Kennedy's already afflicted back. Kennedy directed the rescue of the entire crew and personally rescued three men, one of whom was seriously injured. Kennedy was awarded the Purple Heart for his heroism, and was honorably discharged in 1945.

Father Joe was grooming his son Joe Jr. for political office, but after Joe's tragic death in WWII, John stepped up to the plate to fulfill his father's ambitions. He was elected to the Massachusetts legislature on November 5, 1946. Six years later he was elected to the U.S. Senate. On September 22,1953, he married Jacqueline Lee Bouvier and had two children, Caroline, born November 27, 1957 and John, Jr. born November 25, 1960. In 1954 he had undergone two bouts of back surgery that nearly caused his death. During his recovery he wrote *Profiles in Courage,* which won the Pulitzer Prize for biography in 1957. A stint at the London Clinic ten years earlier confirmed a diagnosis of Addison's Disease, a rare endocrine disorder with a hereditary component. This disease, and Kennedy's other inscrutable medical disorders, were actively kept out the public eye throughout his lifetime. He was usually in chronic pain and was heavily medicated.

Father Joe helped push John F. Kennedy up the political ladder and on July 13, 1960 he was nominated as the Democratic candidate for President. His charismatic personality, charm, and eloquence turned heads on all fronts, and on January 20, 1961, he was sworn in as the 35th President. His inaugural speech mesmerized the nation with the signature phrase, "Ask not what your country can do for you. Ask what you can do for your country." In closing, he addressed humanity across the globe: "Finally, whether you are citizens of America or citizens of the world, ask of us the same high standards of strength and sacrifice which we ask of you." Thus began a sea change in American society. The bygone image of a solid and staid politician was replaced with a philosopher king and Kennedy's administration of The Thousand Days became known as Camelot. He was a charmer, a socialite with show-business connections, notably the "Rat Pack" (which included brother-in-law Peter Lawford, Sinatra, Dean Martin, and Sammy Davis, Jr.), whose Las Vegas acts made Kennedy appear even more debonair. As an icon of popular culture, he and Jackie, his majestic First Lady, lived in a flamboyant style that exceeded their predecessors. Despite his medical problems, he suffered no loss of sexual health, and his legendary woman-izing became increasingly problematic for his administration and for the secret security to contain. Kennedy had it all: wit, brains, style, charisma, good looks, wealth, and power. His was the first televised presidency, and during his Thousand Days defining moments of social revolution transformed the world: the Bay of Pigs, the Cuban Missile Crisis, the Berlin Wall, the first American in outer space, Civil Rights, the threat of nuclear war with the U.S.S.R, Vatican II, nuclear testing, and the Beatles. Kennedy cre-ated the Peace Corps and gave American support to an obscure Southeast Asian nation called Vietnam. But he had enemies in the Right, the CIA, and organized crime. And his charm wore thin.

John F. Kennedy was assassinated at 12:30 PM on Novem-ber 22, 1963, in Dallas, Texas, sending shock waves around the world. Although Lee Harvey Oswald was the convicted assas-sin, many believe J.F.K.'s murder was a conspiracy. His assas-sination was a turning point in American culture, and it marked the end of America's faith in the political establishment.

Camelot was over. It would not return.

The mutual reception by exaltation of Moon and Mercury is clearly represented in Kennedy's life. The Moon (family, the public, one's homeland) and Mercury (siblings, communication, writing, youth, medicine), are shaking hands in evening gloves at a mutual admiration society gala. During his administration Kennedy appointed his brother (Mercury) Robert F. Kennedy as Attorney General and the two were inseparable. His sister

Patricia's marriage to actor Peter Lawford opened the door of the entertainment industry to help facilitate his campaign. There was a history of politics on both sides of his family (Moon), and his father's connections enabled him to move in the highest political and social circles. In *Profiles of Courage,* his literary skill (Mercury) about historical figures (Moon) earned him the Pulitzer Prize. Kennedy was a master orator, (Mercury) whose sterling rhetoric riveted the attention of all nations, and whose popular appeal (Moon) made him a legend in his own time. Medical problems plagued him throughout his life (Virgo), yet his wealthy family (Taurus) provided his every need.

Major Configurations

Determining the distinctions between the view on one's True North, the Midheaven, and the line of least resistance to it (the Principal Planet), one must take into consideration if the Midheaven, its ruler, or Principal Planet is involved in a Major Configuration. If so, it further strengthens the Midheaven and Principal Planet, placing them in a permanent spotlight of success or notoriety. Prominence is attained and held, and these individuals become leaders in their field.

The major configurations with the Midheaven and the Principal Planet used in the Slevin System are the T-square, the Grand Trine, the Grand Cross, and the Yod.

Midheaven as Apex of a T-square

When one's True North is the apex of the powerful T-square, the individual makes an enormous impact on the world at large and remains in the spotlight, whether he or she likes it or not. Seemingly catapulted to the top, if only by default, the world is their oyster and their influence can reach every corner of the globe.

Steven Spielberg's horoscope, shown as Chart 26, provides examples of T-square to Midheaven.

One of the most celebrated and influential American filmmakers and personalities in the history of film, Spielberg is per-

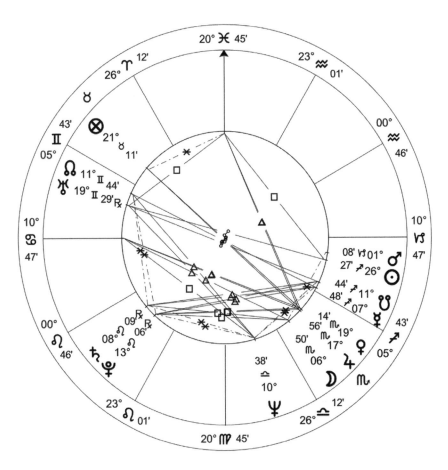

Chart 26. T-square to Midheaven: Steven Spielberg, December 18, 1946, 6:16 PM EST Cincinnati, Ohio 39N09, 84W27.

haps the best known director in the world. Receiving five Oscar nominations and winning two Oscars, his extraordinary use of special effects in *Jaws* (1975), *Close Encounters of the Third Kind* (1977), and *E.T.* (1982), pioneered the emphasis of special effects in both action scenes and in characterization. His landmark use of animated characters in dialogue with humans in *Who Framed Roger Rabbit?* in 1988, along with *Jurassic Park* in 1993, sealed his reputation for blending creativity with technology. Nonetheless, his penetrating insight into the frailties of the human condition in *The Color Purple,* (1985), *Schindler's List* (1993), and *Saving Private Ryan* (1998), earned him critical and universal acclaim.

While growing up in Cincinnati, Spielberg's grandmother tutored Holocaust survivors, whose stories left an indelible impression on the young boy. Spielberg was often the only Jewish student in his classes, and silently endured the jabs of anti-Semitism. Experimenting with his father's camera proved a release valve for the tension in his home. As a child, Spielberg started recording family trips and other events, but soon moved on to filming his own narrative movies. By the time he was twelve years old he actually filmed a movie from a script using a cast of actors. He grew increasingly ambitious and continued to make movies from then on. By the age of 13, Spielberg won a prize for a short war movie he titled *Escape to Nowhere*. Spielberg's first feature length film was a science fiction movie, entitled *Firelight* (1963), which he filmed when he was sixteen. The movie was over two hours long and had a complex plot about an encounter with some aliens—an early foreshadowing of his blockbuster, *Close Encounters of the Third Kind*. His father rented a local movie theater to show the film; in one night it made back the $500 it cost to film it.

Unfortunately, Spielberg's poor high school grades prevented him from entering the UCLA film school. He was rejected twice from the University of Southern California. Eventually, Spielberg entered California State University, but didn't complete his degree for many years. Because California State had no formal film program, he frequently went to the movies and saw every film that he could. He also cajoled his way past the guards at Universal Studios and watched major projects being filmed.

Spielberg continued to make films and prepared a short subject film, *Amblin'*, which he later entered in the 1969 Atlanta Film Festival. It won an award at the Venice Film Festival, and got him a seven-year contract at the studio whose gates he used to crash—Universal—directing television episodes of *Night Gallery*,

Marcus Welby, MD, and TV Movies of the Week, including *Duel* (1971), *Something Evil* (1972), and *Savage* (1973). Today Spielberg uses the name "Amblin'" for his own production company.

The T-square to Spielberg's Midheaven is formed by the opposition of Uranus to the Sun, with Uranus and the Sun squaring the Midheaven. Note Spielberg's Principal Planet is Uranus in his 12th house, which accurately depicts an unusual, inventive person behind the scenes. Uranus rules his 8th house of crisis (wealth and his frequent emphasis on WWII and people in crisis) and (using the Placidus house system) the 9th house of media. Venus ties Uranus as his Principal Planet within one degree. Venus is in detriment, thus it needs help. It gets it through its conjunction to benefic Jupiter, coruler of the Midheaven. Venus rules Spielberg's 5th house of creativity and corules his 11th house of visionary goals, large groups of people, and how he fits into them.

• • •

An example of Ruler of Midheaven as apex of T-square is found in Chart 27 on page 90, Diane von Furstenberg.

This Swiss-American fashion designer, entrepreneur, and author was born Diane Halfin in Belgium to a Jewish mother who was a survivor of Auschwitz. While studying economics at the University of Switzerland in Geneva, she fell in love with German-Italian Prince Egon von Furstenberg, heir to the Fiat fortune. Despite parental disapproval, the couple married on July 16, 1969 and moved to New York, where von Furstenberg debuted her first fashion design show in April 1970. Two children soon followed.

As the wife of a wealthy European prince, Von Furstenberg did not need to earn a living, yet she worked tirelessly in fashion showrooms. Two years later with a $30,000 loan, she opened her own showroom to promote her unique, jersey knit wrap dresses. Her success was overwhelming; orders exceeded over $1 million per month. By 1976, Von Furstenberg sold in excess of 5 million wrap dresses to land covers of *Newsweek* and the *Wall*

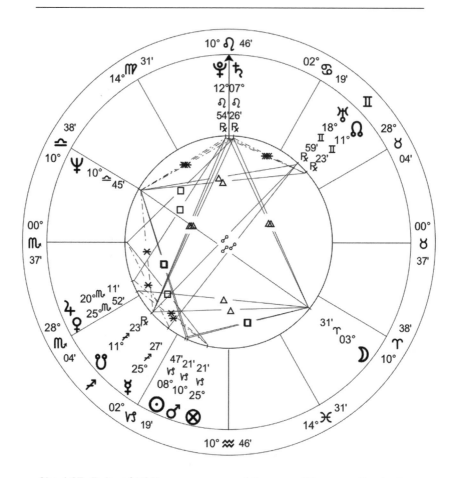

Chart 27. Ruler of Midheaven as apex of T-square: Diane von Furstenberg, December 31, 1946, 3:00 AM MET, Brussels, Belgium. 50N50, 4E20.

Street Journal. Deemed a cultural phenomenon, "The Dress" found its way into almost every American closet and currently hangs in the Smithsonian. Expanding to a full range of products including perfume, cosmetics, eyewear, and luggage, von Furstenberg built her own fashion empire and published *Diane von Furstenberg's Book of Beauty* in 1976. The following year she introduced her Style of Living collection of home furnishings and in 1984 ranked in the top 10 in Savvy magazine's survey of "Top U.S. Businesses Run by Women." A jet-setting socialite, von Furstenberg moved in high-profile circles and lived life in the fast lane. After women's business suits led to the decline of "The Dress," von Furstenberg amicably divorced, sold her dress business and moved to Paris in 1985, where she hosted a literary salon and founded Salvy, a French-language publishing house. She was honored that same year with the New York Mayor's Liberty Medal for citizens of the world who have achieved the American dream. By 1989, her licensed products totaled sales of over $1 billion dollars for the previous decade. Returning to New York in 1992 and resuming control of her business empire, she pioneered television shopping with her creation and on-air selling of her Silk Assets collection, with sales topping $40 million. By 1997 she made a successful comeback to retail with her updated line of signature dresses at Saks Fifth Avenue stores. In her 1998 autobiography, *Diane, A Signature Life,* she wrote, "I lived the American dream. I made money, I made children, I became famous, and I dressed everyone in America."

Von Furstenberg currently manages her New York-based design and marketing studio bearing her name and divides her time between her homes in New York, Connecticut, Paris, and the Bahamas.

Leo rules von Furstenberg's Midheaven, with the Sun, ruler of Leo, in a tight conjunction to Mars at the apex of a T-square between the opposition of the Moon and Neptune. Her Principal Planet, within a one-minute orb, is Neptune, ruling her 5th house of creativity, followed by Pluto in order of exactness, ruling her 2nd house of finance. In keeping with the theory that Outer planets serving as Principal planets make for highly independent careers, Von Furstenberg created her own fashion house (Neptune and the 5th house) and influenced the masses with a product that became a standard (Pluto and the 2nd house). Von Furstenberg studied economics (Pluto) prior to launching her career as a designer. She heard the distant drummer to deviate from a mainstream profession immediately following her show featuring her wrap dress in 1972, when Jupiter was transiting Capricorn conjunct her Sun (ruler Midheaven) and Mars.

Midheaven in a Grand Trine

When the Midheaven is part of a Grand Trine, the individual's potential is noticed, enabled, and promoted by others, often from an early age. They receive and accept valuable training and career assistance to aid in their climb to success, and their rise to the top can appear effortless. The Grand Trine involving the Midheaven smoothes over obstacles on the career path, and these individuals always seem to be in the right place at the right time. Gifted, talented, and fortunate, a drawback is that this group can be inclined to take the course of least resistance, as the Grand Trine bestows good fortune, but with complacency as a constant companion. Initiative, perseverance, and a strong work ethic must be indicated from a strong Mars, Saturn, or other hard aspects.

The horoscope of Gustave Flaubert, Chart 28, provides an example of Midheaven in a Grand Trine.

French author Flaubert is best known for his realist novel *Madame Bovary*. The fifth of six children of Achille Cleophas Bovary and Anne Justine Caroline Fleuriot, Flaubert was raised in a prominent, respected family. His father was chief surgeon at Rouen municipal hospital and his mother, a physician's daughter, descended from ancient Norman families. In delicate health from birth, he was not expected to live to adulthood, however, continuous medical treatment from his father proved successful. A poor student in youth, Flaubert immersed himself in writing and literature and displayed an insatiable curiosity for life and learning. Between the ages of 11 and 14, he wrote many historical works, a play, and philosophical treaties, notably *La Peste à Florence*, in which he laid the groundwork of his rebellion against bourgeois values, sympathy for those in menial positions and disdain for the privileged. At age 20 he left Rouen to study law in Paris, but never completed his second year due to failed examinations, lack of ambition, and a "nervous illness" that was later diagnosed to be epilepsy, an illness he struggled with his whole life. After his father's death in January 1846,

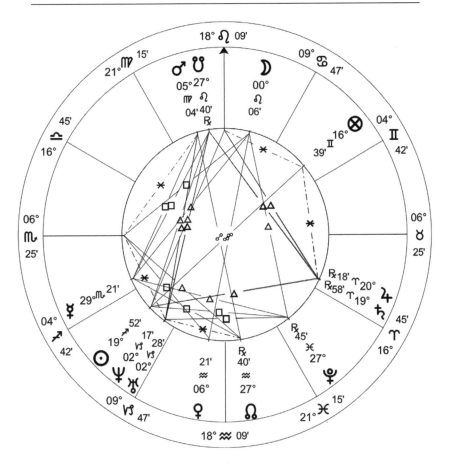

Chart 28. Midheaven in a Grand Trine: Gustave Flaubert, December 12, 1821, 4:00 AM LMT, Rouen, France 49N26, 1E05.

his inheritance enabled him to retire to the family's estate at Croisset, France, where he enjoyed life as a country gentleman of independent means. His picture of domestic bliss included his beloved mother, servant, and adopted niece, all of whom catered to his every need.

After spending 1846–1850 traveling throughout the Mediterranean with pioneer photographer Maxime du Champ, Flaubert returned to Croisset and began to write *Madame Bovary*.

Aiming to write flawless, meticulously chiseled prose, he often labored seven hours a day for many days on a single page in his attempt to achieve perfect composition. "My head reels and throat aches with chasing after, slogging over, delving into, groping after, and bellowing, in a hundred thousand different ways, a sentence that I've finished."[4] Five years later, his literary masterpiece was published. Its realistic depiction of adultery was condemned as immoral, with government action brought against author and publisher. Both were acquitted at trial, and Flaubert subsequently enjoyed success as a writer at the court of Napoleon III and was awarded the Legion of Honor in 1866.

His later novels, *Salammbo* and *Sentimental Education*, were dismissed by most critics, yet other writers revered him, and his impact on literature was profound. Over one hundred and fifty years after its publication, *Madame Bovary* is considered a model of style and is still widely regarded as "the perfect novel."

Despite numerous affairs and a nine-year relationship with poetess Louise Colet, Flaubert never married. Poor health and financial difficulties that arose after his mother's death in 1872 shadowed his later years. In 1875 he gave his fortune to his adored niece to save her husband from bankruptcy.

Flaubert died of a stroke on May 8, 1880, at Croisset. At the time of his death, a press clipping found on his writing desk described him as "one of the uncontested masters of the contemporary novel, perhaps the only one who owes nothing to anyone, and whom everyone else has more or less imitated."

Flaubet's Sun (vitality) and Saturn (hard work) are tied in their positions as Principal Planet. They both trine the Midheaven, forming a Grand Trine in fire, illustrating the extremely fortunate circumstances throughout his domestic life and career, as he never held a job or needed to earn a living. Mars in Virgo in the Midheaven and Saturn in the 6th house, ruling his 3rd house of communication, point to his painstaking attention in achieving the architectural structure of his prose.

The Midheaven in a Grand Cross

Four planets squaring each other within two oppositions creates the Grand Cross, an extremely difficult configuration that gives seemingly endless reserves of drive and stamina to overcome obstacles and achieve results. These classic type-A personalities seek or create challenge, require continuous stimulation and brace themselves for the extreme highs and lows they'll inevitably face, but their endeavors to pull themselves up from their bootstraps are often fraught with hardship. Individuals with a Grand Cross can subsist on raw nerves, sprinting from one crisis to the next, then unravel under frenetic levels of stress. Independent, resilient, and ambitious, they're noticed for their innate capability and strong survivor skills. They take action, command and control and, eventually, they take the grand prize. When the Midheaven is part of the Grand Cross, career, self-promotion, and family matters are their number one priority.

Chart 29 on page 96, Naomi Judd, is an example of Midheaven in a Grand Cross.

This American singer, songwriter, and author was a member of the country and western superstar duo The Judds, consisting of herself and her daughter, Wynonna. During the 1980s they sold over 15 million albums and were the most popular Country Music touring act in the United States. With the outstanding success of winning six Grammys, Country Music's Best Duo Awards for eight consecutive years and 15 Number One singles, their Farewell Concert on December 4, 1991, with six million viewers, was the most successful music event in cable pay-per-view history.

Known as the Cinderella of Country Music for her rags-to-riches story, Judd was barely out of her teens, married, and already a mother of two daughters when she left her loveless marriage. A single mother on welfare with no insurance, she survived on minimum wage jobs across America, often living without the basic amenities of heat, indoor plumbing, and telephone while doggedly pursuing a nursing degree on government

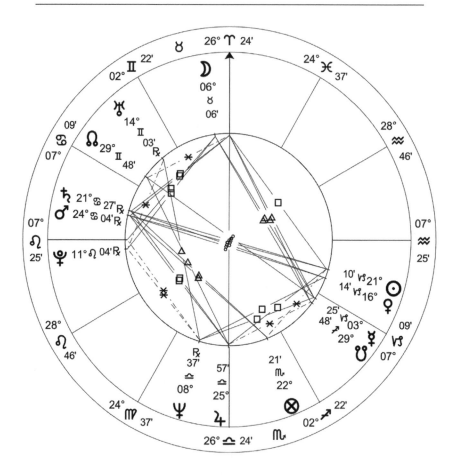

Chart 29. Midheaven in a Grand Cross: Naomi Judd, January 11, 1946, 6:45 PM Ashland, Kentucky, 38N28, 82S38.

loans, all while raising two distinctively talented children. Judd fanatically encouraged her oldest daughter Wynonna's musical talent, singing harmony to deflect Wynonna's extreme shyness. Heads turned at their sound. A pleasant pastime evolved into a full-time obsession; The Judds performed anywhere they could, promoted by ever-enterprising Naomi.

Following the country music trail to Nashville, The Judds auditioned for a music executive on March 2, 1983. One hour later they had a record deal and began their meteoric rise to international fame. The Judds became a household word and were the "stars next door," spending hours socializing with their fans after each performance, cultivating lasting friendships and a legion of followers. Naomi and Wynonna were at the pinnacle of their career as international superstars, daughter Ashley was successfully launching an acting career in Hollywood, when disaster struck. In March 1990, Naomi was diagnosed with hepatitis C, a disease she had contracted while working as a nurse in the intensive care unit. Debilitated, she performed for another year on medication, formally retiring at the Farewell Concert on December 4, 1991.

Judd retired to her farm in Tennessee, trying alternative methods of healing and rekindling her deep faith. She spent three years convalescing and writing her best selling autobiography *Love Can Build a Bridge,* which was subsequently made into a television miniseries with herself as coproducer. Founding the Naomi Judd Research and Education Fund for Hepatitis Research, she has raised over one million dollars to help find a cure for Hepatitis. In remission since 1993, she has emerged as a champion for alternative methods of healing, restoration of the family and national health care reform, speaking at high-profile summits and Capitol Hill hearings. A poster woman for the American dream, her unique ability to bridge the gap between academics and everyday people with down to earth delivery and homespun wisdom ensures her mass appeal, laced with humility: "I'm not an expert at anything, except making mistakes, but I do have a Ph.D. from the school of hard knocks and I'm a road scholar. America is my research lab and I'm just a student of human nature."[5]

Jupiter, at the apex of Judd's T-square between the Sun and Venus and Saturn and Mars, opposes the Midheaven within one degree, creating a Grand Cross in Cardinal signs. This dynamic configuration illustrates Judd's profile of an independent and energetic high achiever, able to initiate action and overcome obstacles with tireless pursuit.

The Midheaven in a Yod

A Yod, also called a double quincunx, is formed when two planets are in sextile to each other and are both quincunx a third planet. This atypical aspect creates a mechanism of fine-tuning, coupled with a fated sense of destiny. Yod is the Hebrew word for hand and, traditionally, the Yod is a minor aspect defined as the "Hand of God." The apex of a Yod operates with the high-frequency sensitivity of a dowsing rod that inexplicably rearranges circumstances, enabling the individual to detect resources, intangible to others, that influence their fate and often the fate of those around them. As the dowser from antiquity possessed the power to find water underground to sustain life for themselves and their village, individuals with this aspect have a heightened awareness that discerns peculiar subtleties, creating breakthroughs for themselves and others.

Chart 30 is an example of the Midheaven as apex of a Yod, the horoscope of Christa McAuliffe, American teacher and astronaut, the first civilian selected to travel to outer space in NASA spacecraft *Challenger*.

The first of five children born to Grace and Ed Corrigan, Sharon Christa's sunny, contributive nature showed early as her mother's constant companion in helping to raise her younger siblings. An excellent student with a high IQ, she met Steve McAuliffe in high school and, after graduating Framingham State College with a degree in history in 1970, married him on August 23, 1970. The couple moved to Washington D.C. where Steve studied law at Georgetown University and Christa taught American history in suburban Maryland. Her son Scott was born in September 1976. Two years later McAuliffe earned a master's degree in Education Administration from Bowie State College in Maryland. That same year the couple moved to Concord, New Hampshire where Steve accepted a position as an assistant to the state attorney general.

After the birth of their daughter Caroline in 1979, Christa stayed home to raise her family and immersed herself in the

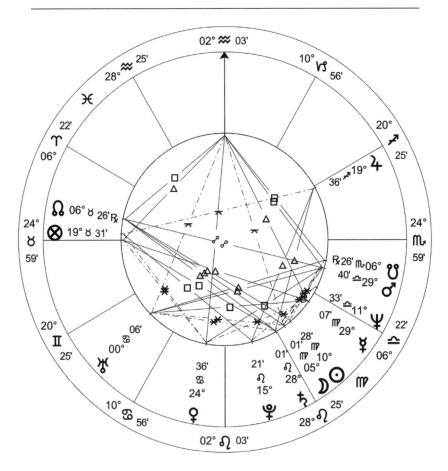

Chart 30. Midheaven as apex of a Yod: Christa McAuliffe, September 2, 1948. 10:13 PM EDT, Boston, MA 42N21 71W03.

community efforts of Girl Scout leader, day care center worker and fund-raiser for her church and local hospital. By 1982 she was teaching social studies in Concord High School where she became known as "The Field Trip Teacher," believing that learning is best when it is experiential and hands-on. By all accounts she was an outstanding instructor and mentor to her students. Every summer she participated in a program called A Better Chance, adopting an underprivileged child into her family. When a suicidal teenager called her one night, McAuliffe invited her to stay at her home, where she watched the girl sleep safely until morning.

When NASA advertised for the first American private citizen to enter outer space and communicate the experience back to earth everyone thought Christa the perfect candidate. On the eleven-page application she wrote, "I remember being in my home when the first satellites were launched. My parents were amazed and I was caught up in their wonder. I remember when Alan Shepard made his historic flight—not even an orbit—and I was thrilled. I watched the Space Age being born and I would like to participate."

NASA was seeking an ordinary person to do the extraordinary: teach lessons from space. McAuliffe was selected on July 19, 1985 from over 11,000 applicants, including doctors, scholars, and research scientists. Intensive training followed and, after extended delays due to multiple technical difficulties, the spacecraft *Challenger* lifted off on January 28, 1986 at 11:39 AM EST. One minute and 18 seconds later, at 42,000 feet and traveling at the speed of 2,000 miles an hour, the *Challenger* exploded. There were no survivors.

The Yod in McAuliffe's chart is formed by the double quincunx of the Moon and Uranus to her Midheaven. Another way to find Yods is to locate the midpoint of a sextile, then note the degree 180 degrees opposite that midpoint for the degree that completes the Yod. For example, the Moon in Virgo and Uranus in Cancer in McAuliffe's chart are in a sextile aspect, the midpoint of which could be anywhere between 0 and 5 Degrees of Leo. Any degree at 0–5 degrees of Aquarius, 180 degrees opposite the midpoint, creates the apex of the Yod. In this case McAuliffe's Midheaven at 2 degrees Aquarius forms the apex. She applied to NASA for her unparalleled position while transiting Jupiter was crossing her Midheaven, triggering her Yod and rearranging her priorities. Thus she would have an unusual, futuristic (Aquarius) career change (Midheaven transit), involving travel and education (Jupiter) that would ultimately effect her unprecedented destiny.

• • •

The horoscope of Carl Jung, Chart 31 on page 102, provides an example of Ruler of Midheaven as Apex of Yod.

Swiss psychiatrist, author, and founder of modern analytical psychiatry, Jung was author of many books, including *Modern Man in Search of a Soul* (1933), *Synchronicity* (1955), *Undiscovered Self* (1958), *Memories, Dreams, Reflections* (1963), and *Man and His Symbols* (1964). In the field of psychology named after him, Jung pioneered the theories that have evolved into common parlance and usage, namely synchronicity, individuation, archetypes, animus, anima, personal and collective unconscious, introvert, extravert, complex, personal myth, and personality types, the codification of which led to the popular Myers-Briggs test. In his field of analytical psychology, the most important and lifelong task of any person is fulfillment through the process of individuation, the achievement of harmony of conscious and unconscious, which makes a person one and whole.

Jung was the fourth born, first surviving, and only son of Paul Achilles Jung, an impoverished Swiss country pastor and his troubled, unstable wife Emilie Preiswerk. Each parent was the thirteenth child in their families, with both sides replete with physicians and ministers. His mother's patrician family had a strong interest in the occult, holding séances on Saturday nights. Many members of his maternal extended family, including Emilie, possessed what they referred to as personality number 1 and personality number 2. This latter personality was a trance state that produced visions and spirits. Emilie's personality number 2 often became her dominant mode, as she isolated herself and talked to spirits throughout the night. Frequently hospitalized for her disturbing behavior, Jung felt her absence deeply, thus beginning his "feeling of the feminine as one of natural unreliability, one can never rely upon it."[6] During these times the dark-haired, olive-skinned maid became Jung's caregiver, and it was she who became his basis for the

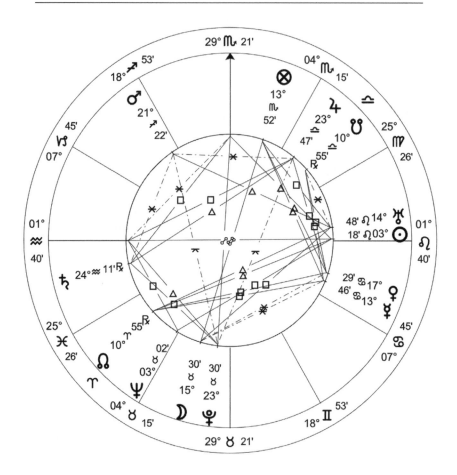

Chart 31. Ruler of Midheaven as Apex of Yod. Example: Carl Jung, July 26, 1875, 7:32 PM, Kesswill, Switzerland, 47N36, 9E20.

anima and the feminine mysterious. Jung's solitary childhood was spent listening to his father's sermons with deep skepticism and reveling in the wonders of nature with his mother when she was home as personality number 1. In his early youth he blended his parents' ideologies, believing that the spirit of God was reflected in humankind, in the natural world, and in the cosmos. At age 12, when fainting spells from a head injury kept him out of school, he communed with nature, sculpted, drew and, above all, "was able to plunge into the world of the mysterious."[7]

Jung attended the University of Basel on money borrowed from a paternal uncle, completing all academic and medical studies in just five years. He wrote his dissertation on séances, titled *On Psychology and Pathology of So-Called Occult Phenomena*. After passing his physician examination on December 10, 1900, he was employed as a second level assistant physician at the Psychiatric University Hospital and Clinic of Zurich. On February 14, 1903 he married Emma Rauschenbach, the second-wealthiest heiress in Switzerland who, despite Jung's numerous affairs, remained his faithful confidante for fifty-three years. By 1904 he had a thriving private practice and was lecturing on psychiatry at the University of Zurich. In 1906 he published a book on *Dementia Praecox* (schizophrenia) that established him as a scholar of international repute. After meeting Sigmund Freud on March 3, 1907, Freud pronounced Jung "my scientific son and heir."[8] They joined forces in their analyses of sexuality, the unconscious, and dreams, presenting their work on a lecture tour of the United States in 1911. Jung's formal break with Freud occurred the following year with his revolutionary book *The Psychology of the Unconscious*, which disagreed with the Freudian emphasis on sexual anguish as the root of all neurosis and the literal interpretation of the Oedipal complex.

An intermittent professor at the Universities of Zurich and Basel, Jung spent decades traveling the globe studying mythology, tribes, cults, rituals, customs, and religion. His private practice attracted an international clientele of patients, students, devotees, and hangers-on. "My life has been permeated and held together by one idea and one goal, namely to penetrate the secret of the personality. Everything can be explained from this central point, and all my works relate to this one theme."[9] He died on June 6, 1961 in Zurich.

Pluto, co-ruler of Jung's Midheaven, is the apex of a Yod between Mars and Jupiter. Using the Midheaven as ruler of the mother, the Yod points to the mother's interest in occult phenomenon and to Jung's own heightened awareness. His entire career could be compared to a dowsing rod that detected hidden resources and discerned intrinsic subtleties in the human condition.

Chapter 4

THE CARDINAL AXIS

*In every field of endeavor he that is first must
perpetually live in the white light of publicity.*
THEODORE F. MACMANUS

The planet Earth rotates in the style of a gyroscope, and the
seasons of the year are caused by the 23.5 degree tilt of its
axis. The top of Earth's axis is continuously pointed toward a
position in space near the North Star while it revolves around
the Sun. During the first half of the year the northern hemisphere
is more exposed to the Sun than the southern hemisphere. In the
second half of the year, the southern hemisphere receives more
exposure. In the northern hemisphere the Sun's position in the
sky at noon is higher during summer than it is during winter.
The day the Sun reaches its highest elevation occurs on the day
with the most hours of daylight, usually occurring on June 21st.
This day is called the summer solstice. "Solstice" is a combination of two Latin words, *Sol*, meaning Sun, and *sistere*, meaning
to stand still. The Sun reaches its lowest elevation at noon on
December 21st, which marks the winter solstice. Solstice positions and dates are reversed in the southern hemisphere. These
all-important days played a highly significant role in the lives

of our ancestors, and rightly so, for it represented the life and death cycle of the Sun, the giver of life.

In ancient times, human subsistence was contingent upon the success of the growing season. Winter proved a difficult time for prehistoric peoples whose growing season had ended; the weather turned colder, the days grew shorter and the life-giving Sun sank lower in the sky. With survival dictated by the elements, tribes were forced to live off stored provisions and whatever animals they could hunt. Fearing the Sun would disappear and leave them in permanent darkness, aboriginal peoples gave thanks when they saw the Sun "stand still" and then strengthen, giving longer days and renewed prospects of the coming growing season. It called for celebration. Fires were lit, food was served and the merry-making held forth. Note that the Summer and winter solstices mark the changing of the seasons and occur in Cardinal signs. The word Cardinal stems from the Latin root *cardo*, meaning hinge, or turning point.

So, what does this have to do with a horoscope? The answer is, Plenty. Solstice points, also known as 0 degrees of the signs Cancer and Capricorn, serve as hinges, or turning points, in astronomy and astrology. As they mark the highest points of the Sun as it orbits the ecliptic, so planets and angles on these degrees mark the highest points of personal exposure. These points are not to be confused with the Midheaven. The Midheaven is the highest point of visibility in the horoscope and everybody has one, but not everyone has a planet or angle on the Cardinal Axis. These degrees are highly energized. They attract attention to themselves and will create headline notoriety. Like it or not, a planet or angle on this degree will get you noticed and catapult you into the forefront. Our ancestors celebrated these points on the ecliptic and so will you, once you discover them, because *the more degrees a horoscope has on the Cardinal Axis, the more celebrated and high profile the personality will be. The Cardinal Axis is the World Stage.*

While 0 Cancer and 0 Capricorn serve as the Solstice Points that mark the Cardinal Axis, these two degrees are not the only ones that lay claim to all the fun and notoriety. The others are 22 degrees, 30 minutes Cardinal, 15 degrees Fixed, and 7 degrees, 30 minutes Mutable. The reasoning behind these degrees sharing the Cardinal Axis is as follows:

Astrology is the language of the Universe as systematized by planets, math, and measurement. The ecliptic is a circle, and the measurement of all circles is 360 degrees. Divisions of this circle are broken down in to what are known as harmonics. For example, the second harmonic is 360 divided by 2, which equals 180 degrees. Note that 0 degrees Cancer and 0 degrees Capricorn are 180 degrees apart, also known as being in opposition. This aspect produces *tension*. The third harmonic is 360 divided by 3, which equals 120 degrees. This is the trine aspect, which produces *ease*. The Fourth harmonic is 360 divided by 4, which equals 90 degrees, determining the square aspect, which determines *action*. The fourth harmonic is the one astrologers use to determine the "hard angles" in a horoscope. These are the angles that signify action, which manifests into events and periods of high productivity, for better or worse, in the person's life. As the square always produces action, so do its smaller components.

- 90 degrees divided by 2 = 45 degrees. This is the semisquare.
- 45 degrees divided by 2 = 22 degrees, 30 minutes. This is the semi-semisquare
- A sesqui-quadrate, or a sesquare = 135 degrees, or a square and a half.
- 135 divided by 2 = 67 degrees, 30 minutes. This is the semi-sesquare.

Thus all components of 2 and 4, or the second and fourth harmonic, are energized on the Cardinal Axis as illustrated in the degrees above.

Here's another simpler way of looking at it. To begin, the zodiac is converted into 360-degree notation as follows:

0 degrees–30 degrees = Aries, a Cardinal sign
30 degrees–60 degrees = Taurus, a Fixed sign
60 degrees–90 degrees = Gemini, a Mutable sign
90 degrees–120 degrees = Cancer, a Cardinal sign
120 degrees–150 degrees = Leo, a Fixed sign
150 degrees–180 degrees = Virgo, a Mutable sign
180 degrees–210 degrees = Libra, a Cardinal sign
210 degrees–240 degrees = Scorpio, a Fixed sign
240 degrees–270 degrees = Sagittarius, a Mutable sign
270 degrees–300 degrees = Capricorn, a Cardinal sign
300 degrees–330 degrees = Aquarius, a Fixed sign
330 degrees–360 degrees = Pisces, a Mutable sign

Starting at 0 degrees, add the semi-semisquare, 22 degrees, 30 minutes throughout the zodiac:

- 0 + 22 degrees, 30 minutes = 22 degrees, 30 minutes Aries
- 22 degrees, 30 minutes of Aries + 22 degrees, 30 minutes = 45 degrees, or 15 degrees of Taurus.
- 45 degrees + 22 degrees, 30 minutes = 67 degrees, 30 minutes, or 7 degrees Gemini, 30 minutes.
- 67 degrees, 30 minutes + 22 degrees, 30 minutes = 90 degrees, or 0 degrees of Cancer.
- And so forth through all 360 degrees.
- Thus any degree at 0 degrees or 22 degrees, 30 minutes of any Cardinal sign will be on the Cardinal Axis
- Any degree at 15 degrees of any Fixed sign is on the Cardinal Axis
- Any degree at 7 degrees, 30 minutes of any Mutable sign is on the Cardinal Axis

If the Midheaven is your point of highest visibility and the Principal Planet is how you move the goods to reach your summit, a planet or angle on the Cardinal Axis will catapult you into the public eye. For example, if you have Saturn at 0 degrees of any Cardinal sign, 22 degrees, 30 minutes of any Cardinal sign,

15 degrees of any Fixed sign, or 7 degrees, 30 minutes of any Mutable sign, you're already noticed for being a very responsible, hard-working citizen who is very prominent in your chosen field. Your front and center status could be as a CEO or on the front page of the local newspaper as president of the PTA. The Cardinal Axis does not confer decency or wealth on the part of the individual, just high profile recognition, whether good or bad. Your efforts will attract attention to themselves and you'll receive headline attention whether you want it or not. A well-aspected Midheaven can secure you prime location in the marketplace. A Midheaven on the Cardinal Axis can put you in Times Square, right in the epicenter of commerce. An orb of one degree is permitted on either side of the Cardinal Axis, which is also known as the World Axis or Aries Point.

The Cardinal Axis speaks for itself. A planet or angle exactly conjunct it has a pulsing, electrifying impact that connects one to the world at large, the feeling one gets when standing in the middle of Times Square. The one-degree orb is still strong enough to feel its intensity, akin to being one block away from Times Square. Can you feel the difference?

An example of Midheaven conjunct the Cardinal Axis can be found in Chart 32 on page 110, the horoscope of Joan Baez, American folksinger, songwriter, author, and political activist who held the pulse of Sixties radicalism from its inception. In an impassioned soprano voice Joan Baez sang the ballads, led the protests, mentored the counterculture, championed the disadvantaged, and introduced the world to a singing poet named Bob Dylan. Her forty-year musical career is inseparable from her activism toward moral courage, social justice, and world peace.

Joan Baez was the middle daughter of Mexican-born physicist Albert Baez and Edinburgh-born drama professor Joan Bridge, both of whom were Quakers. Albert refused lucrative jobs to protest war. The family moved frequently due to his frequent change of jobs, taking them across the United States, France, Switzerland, and Italy. In 1951 they lived in Baghdad

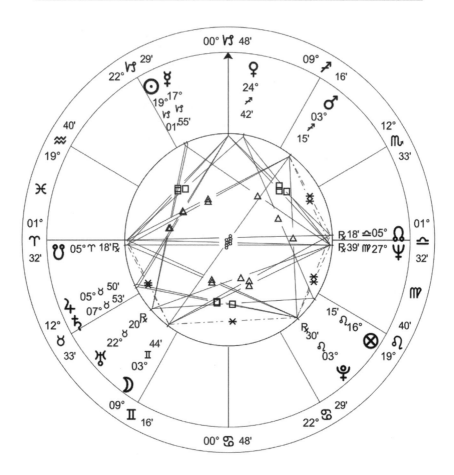

Chart 32. Midheaven conjunct the Cardinal Axis: Joan Baez, January 9, 1941, 10:45 AM EST Staten Island, NY 40N35, 74W09.

for a year, where the abject poverty and inhumane treatment of the population left an indelible impression on young Joan. Her musical talent showed early, she sang in choirs, and learned to play the ukulele and the guitar.

Accepting a faculty position at MIT, Albert Baez moved his family to Boston, where Joan studied drama at Boston University. Cambridge was the center of the folk music scene and Joan played in local coffeehouses, colleges, and concert halls to critical acclaim. Her big break came in 1959 at the Newport Folk Festival, where the angel-voiced, barefoot teenager won rave reviews and was signed to a record label. The following year her first solo album, *Joan Baez* (1960), was a huge success, followed by three subsequent albums that went gold. By the mid-1960s Baez emerged as a spearhead of the American roots revival, touring throughout America from 1961–1963 with her folksinging colleague and lover Bob Dylan. After hearing Dr. Martin Luther King's powerful appeals for justice, Baez swiftly gave many southern performances for Civil Rights, culminating in her album *Joan Baez in Concert* (1962) which earned a Grammy nomination. By 1965, Baez was not only the quintessential female folksinger emulated by every Baby Boomer female who ever picked up an acoustic guitar, she was also the poster woman of protest. After founding the Institute of Non-Violence in 1965, Baez refused to pay taxes that funded the Vietnam War, and encouraged her audiences nationwide to follow suit. In 1967 she did two stints in jail for her antiwar protests.

On March 23, 1968, Baez married fellow Vietnam protestor David Harris; their son Gabriel was born the following year. Appearing at the legendary Woodstock Festival in August 1969 gave her an international podium for her music and her politics; her performance of "The Ballad of Joe Hill" was a paean to protesting workers.

Baez launched a world tour in the 70s, espousing political causes and non-violence at every venue. She visited Vietnam, sang Christmas carols and delivered mail to American soldiers, worked in refugee camps on the Thai border, and helped establish the U.S. branch of Amnesty International in Southeast Asia. While touring Italy, she paid homage to the Italian-American radicals, Sacco and Vanzetti. Her version of "The Night They Drove Old Dixie Down" was a top ten hit. The '80s found her seeking to improve human rights in South America, visiting with Mothers of the Disappeared in Argentina in 1981. Despite her presence, authorities in Chile, Brazil, and Argentina forbade her to perform, fearing her public criticism of their human rights abuses would reach mass audiences. Her very appearance posed a threat to their government.

In 1985 Baez opened the Live Aid concert in Philadelphia. She published her autobiography *And a Voice to Sing With* two years later. After thirty albums and forty years in the spotlight, she still tours on behalf of Amnesty International and other causes.

In August 2005 Baez appeared at the Iraq War protest outside President Bush's ranch in Texas. Her message is pure: "My devotion to nonviolence and social change formed long before I picked up a ukulele and will go on until I fall into the grave."

Baez's Midheaven at 0 degrees of the Cardinal Axis catapulted her into front-and center recognition as a teenager, and her career in the public eye has never waned. Singing at almost every high-profile public protest for nearly every peaceful cause, her presence, voice, and politics have reached every corner of the globe. While her Principal Planet is Jupiter, her Midheaven at 0 degrees Cardinal overrides it in the search for individual success. Jupiter helped spread her benevolent philosophy, but the Cardinal Axis speaks for itself. A high-profile career is a given. The goods don't need to be moved. They're already in the spotlight.

• • •

An example of Principal Planet on the Cardinal Axis is found in the horoscope of Benito Mussolini, Chart 33.

Mussolini was a fascist dictator and Prime Minister of Italy from 1922–1943 who lead his country into World War II on the side of Nazi Germany.

Benito Amilcare Andrea Mussolini was the oldest son of Alessandro Mussolini, a blacksmith and ardent socialist, and Rosa Maltoni, a deeply religious schoolteacher. Named Benito after Mexican revolutionary Benito Juarez, Mussolini was a problematic and violent child. By age eleven he was banned from his mother's church and expelled from school for stabbing a fellow student and throwing an inkpot at a teacher. Despite his boor-

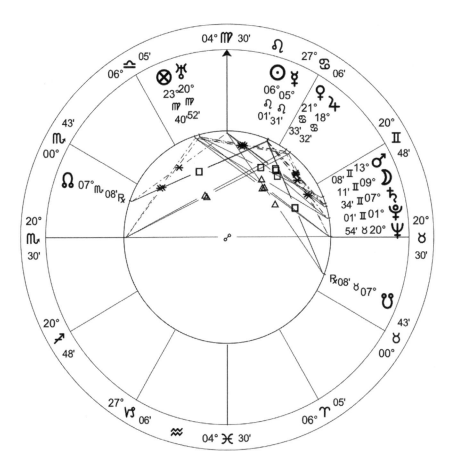

Chart 33. Principal Planet on the Cardinal Axis: Benito Mussolini, July 29, 1883, 1:10 PM GMT, Forli, Dovia Il Predappio, Italy, 44N13, 12E02.

ish behavior he was a quick study and an avid writer who followed in his father's socialist footsteps. At 18 he became qualified as an elementary teacher, a position he held sporadically from 1906–1909, while he published and edited two socialist newspapers, becoming Italy's foremost political activist. When Italy declared war on Libya in 1911, Mussolini called for a general strike, was arrested, and imprisoned for preaching pacifist propaganda. Upon his release, he moved to Milan as the appointed editor of Italy's primary Socialist newspaper *Avanti*, where he was a staunch advocate of insurrection and authoritarian rule.

During World War I, Mussolini joined the pro-allied interventionists and the Nationalist party. The Socialist party, opposed to all participation in national wars, fired him from *Avanti* for supporting the Nationalists. In 1914, Mussolini founded his own newspaper, the *Popolo di Italia*, along with the pro-war group Fasci di Azione Rivoluzionaria, to encourage Italy's entrance into the war on the allied side. After Italy entered World War I, he married his common-law wife, Donna Rachele Guidi, on August 31, 1915 and entered the Italian army that same day. Rising to the rank of corporal, he was wounded during grenade practice in 1917 and returned to Milan to edit his newspaper, which would later become the ideological mouthpiece of his Fascist regime.

At the end of World War I, Mussolini switched military allegiances. Believing the Marxist tenet that social revolution is a result of war, he formally organized the disgruntled veterans into the Fasci de Combattimento on February 23, 1919, as a reaction to the failure of laissez-faire economics. Thus Fascism was born. The word "fascism" stemmed from the Italian *fasces*, or bundle. The party's insignia was the ancient Roman bundle of rods bound together around an ax with the blade projecting, carried before ancient Roman magistrates as an emblem of authority. The Fascisti, in uniforms of black shirts, stood for fierce nationalism and were in violent opposition to communism and socialism. In 1920 the lira fell, resulting in nationwide panic. Amid the social, economic, cultural, and parliamentary breakdown of post-war Italy, Mussolini encouraged coercive reformation while his Black Shirts, as they became known, became champions of law and order, practicing armed terrorism and murder on all radical and progressive groups. The Black Shirts, organized in the same chain of command as the ancient Roman legion with the Roman salute, culminated the Fascist party's takeover with their march on Rome on October 28, 1922. King Victor Emmanuele II allowed them to remain in the city and called on Mussolini, still in Milan, to form a new government, as Fascism was Italy's last hope to avoid an imminent civil war between communists and socialists. Mussolini disassembled the existing democratic government in Italy between 1920–1921 and replaced it with his Fascist regime, controlling all media and military action.

As prime minister, Mussolini enforced strict censorship and altered the rules of election so that by 1926 all other political parties in Italy were dissolved. Assuming dictatorial power in his role of *Il Duce* (the leader), he presented himself as the superhuman commander in chief whose primary ambition was to restore "the order and power of the old Roman Empire." After he seized control of the ministries of the interior, foreign affairs, colonies, corporations, armed forces, and public works, Italy soon became a police state. His bombastic rhetoric, full of contradiction and inaccuracy, persuaded the Italian public that he was the superhuman dictator who could solve all problems of economics and government. A master of propaganda, intimidation, and strict censorship, Mussolini implemented his experience in journalism by enforcing the Press Laws in 1925, which stated that all journalists must be registered as Fascists. Virtually every form of media, press, radio, education and film were systematically biased to create the impression that Fascism was the new order of Italy. Teachers and newspapers editors had to swear an oath to defend the Fascist regime. Fascist foreign policy was a model of aggressive nationalism, with military invasions prior to World War II against Greece, Libya, Albania, and Ethiopia facilitating Mussolini's campaign of recreating the ancient Roman image of the Mediterranean of *mare nostrum* ("our sea" in Latin). In 1940 the overconfident dictator declared war on Britain, France, the Soviet Union, and the United States, suffering crushing defeats on all fronts. These debacles resulted in Italy being a target for attacks from the allied forces, especially the successful Anglo-American landing in Sicily in 1943, which caused Mussolini's cabinet members to denounce him at the Fascist Grand Council on July 25, 1943. King Victor

Emmanuel stripped Mussolini of his power. He was arrested and kept in isolation at a mountain retreat. Rescued by German paratroopers in a spectacular raid, Mussolini fled to Gargnano in northern Italy, where in 1944 he set up the Republic of Salo, a Fascist puppet state. Fascist leaders who had abandoned Il Duce were executed, including his son-in-law.

When German power collapsed in April 1945, Italian partisans captured Mussolini and his mistress, Clareta Petaci, on April 27th, while both were escaping in disguise to Switzerland. Mussolini was executed the following day. Clareta threw herself in front of her lover, taking a bullet with him. They were hung upside down in Piazzale Loreto, Milan, where crowds gathered to spit on their corpses.

Saturn on the Cardinal Axis as Mussolini's Principal Planet signified his potent, compelling impact in the public eye, complete with emulation of a historical tradition. Its angular placement in Gemini reinforces high visibility with an inclination toward journalism, teaching, distinctive expression, and a connection to siblings. When Mussolini was on campaign, he gave his crucial editorial seat to his brother Arnaldo. Moreover, the tireless tyrant wrote three books, *John Hus, the Veracious* (1913), *The Cardinal's Mistress* (1928), and *My Rise and Fall* (1944).

Chapter 5

_____

APPEARANCES COUNT

Talent counts 30 percent. Appearance counts 70.
ANONYMOUS

While the Midheaven symbolizes one's public presentation, the Ascendant represents one's personal presentation. The ascendant is the lens through which one's whole world is viewed, combined with one's early conditioning and overall physical appearance. When the Ascendant or its ruler is conjunct the Cardinal Axis it overrides the power of the Principal Planet. It holds a power all its own. The person's personality, physical appearance, or physical attributes are crucial components that project them into the public eye. Performers, athletes, and models trade on these very commodities for success. Their very presence is their stock in trade. Their faces, bodies, or physical attributes command instant attention and are skillfully utilized as finely tuned instruments to reach the summit. The image is their icon and they cannot "phone it in." Often there were unusual circumstances in the early environment that got them headline attention, whether they sought it or not. The Cardinal Axis in connection to the Ascendant places one's physical presence and

_____

unique individualities in neon lights, all ready to be placed in Times Square, for it goes without saying that they'll be the center of attraction.

Audrey Hepburn, Chart 34, provides an example of Ascendant coruler conjunct Cardinal Axis.

Hepburn wass the Belgian dancer and actress who catapulted from the ranks of chorus dancer to international stardom with an Academy Award in 1953 for her first lead role in the film classic, *Roman Holiday*. That same year she won a Tony for her stage performance in the play *Ondine*, in which she played a water nymph who leaves her native element and trespasses on the alien territory of mortal man. It was a role for which she was impeccably cast.

Despite talent and a tenacious work ethic, much of Audrey Hepburn's mass appeal was in her exquisitely distinctive appearance. With "brows that already slanted toward the Orient,"[1] her featherweight, elfin looks gave her an ethereal beauty all her own. Film director Billy Wilder once recalled, "You looked around and suddenly there was this dazzling creature looking like a wide-eyed doe prancing in the forest. Everybody on the set was in love within five minutes."[2]

The wild-eyed doe defied description in Hollywood. As the antithesis of the buxom blonde pin-up star, the human Bambi with aristocratic bearing and an indefinable accent created a new definition of chic that has been plagiarized yet never rewritten.

The only daughter of English/Irish banker Anthony Hepburn-Ruston and Dutch Baroness Ella Van Heemstra, Hepburn, then called Edda, enjoyed an idyllic early childhood in Brussels with her two half brothers from her mother's previous marriage. Her mother's strict discipline differed widely from her father's dashing, easy-going charm, and when he left the family forever after a marital row in 1935, 6-year-old Audrey was devastated. The Baroness soon moved with her children to her ancestral home in Arnhem, Holland, where shy, reserved Audrey attended school and rigorously pursued ballet.

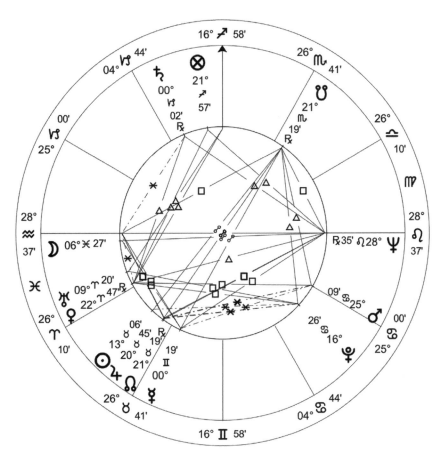

Chart 34. Ascendant coruler conjunct Cardinal Axis: Audrey Hepburn, May 4, 1929, 3:00 AM BST Brussels, Belgium, 50N50 4E22.

The outbreak of World War II impacted Arnhem almost immediately. The German occupation closed the ballet school, but Audrey and other undeterred students set up a makeshift school behind curtains. In an effort to raise money for the Dutch Resistance, Mother Ella organized amateur dance performances after which the audience passed the hat. Audrey distributed copies of radio dispatches and leaflets on anti-Nazism carried in her shoes and once, due to her command of English, carried a message to a fallen British paratrooper hiding in the woods. She witnessed Jewish families boarding trains to destinations unknown and saw her beloved Uncle escorted away by the Gestapo for questioning, never to return.

By 1944, citizens of Arnhem were on starvation rations of one meal a day. There was no fuel, candles, soap or safe drinking water. Already malnourished and anemic, Hepburn, often bedridden due to hunger and weakness, developed edema that swelled her legs and feet so that ballet became a thing of the past. After the Battle of Arnhem in September 1944, the remaining inhabitants of the town were ordered to evacuate by 8 AM the following morning or be shot. Hepburn joined the 100,000 townspeople who were marched into the open countryside to fend for themselves. The resourceful baroness found refuge in a house previously owned by her grandfather in a nearby village, where the starving refugees ate raw roots and flower bulbs. While searching for food in Arnhem in the closing weeks of the war, Hepburn hid in the cellar of a ruined house to avoid capture by German soldiers. Her absence was long enough to convince her mother that her daughter was taken when, seeing Hepburn limp home, Ella's joy was eclipsed by Hepburn's emaciated condition. In addition to anemia and edema, Hepburn had developed jaundice. Immediately after Holland's liberation, Mother and daughter moved to Amsterdam where Hepburn was hospitalized.

After moving to London in late 1948, Hepburn worked as a dancer, interpreter, and model. By 1951 she was playing bit parts in films. During a break in filming on location in Monte Carlo Hepburn was dancing on the beach where aged author Colette was being pushed along the seafront in her wheelchair. She pointed at Hepburn saying, *Voila ma Gigi.* Introductions were made, contracts signed, and on November 24, 1951, Hepburn made her Broadway debut in *Gigi.* Rave reviews garnered her next plum role in the film *Roman Holiday*, for which she won the Academy Award on March 24, 1954. Her career soared. She made twenty-five films, including *Sabrina* (1954), *Funny Face*

(1957), *The Nun's Story* (1959) *Breakfast at Tiffany's* (1961), and *My Fair Lady* (1964), effecting Cinderella transformations in each role. Fashion designer Hubert de Givenchy created a definitive style for her that was copied internationally. At 5 feet 7 inches, Hepburn had a twenty-inch waist and never weighed more than 110 pounds.

Hepburn married actor Mel Ferrer in 1954. She had one son, Sean, in 1960, after five miscarriages. After the marriage ended in 1968, she married Italian psychiatrist Andrea Dotti the following year. Her second son Luca was born in 1969 after a pregnancy of total bed rest. Her marriage to Dotti ended in 1982.

In 1988 Hepburn was appointed a special ambassador to United Nations Children's Fund (UNICEF). As a survivor of war and its deprivations of hunger she dedicated the remainder of her life to aid impoverished children in the poorest nations of the world in Asia, Africa, Central and South America. Serving the needy in squalor, she mirrored her favorite role of Sister Luke in *The Nun's Story*. In her later years she became known for her outstanding humanitarian service as much for her acting career.

She died of colon cancer on January 23, 1993.

Saturn, coruler of Hepburn's Aquarius Ascendant, is exactly conjunct the Cardinal Axis in the 10th house within a 3 minute orb. Her physical appearance thrust her into the public eye in an acting career of international renown, followed by a second high-profile vocation with UNICEF.

● ● ●

An example of Ascendant conjunct Cardinal Axis is found in the horoscope of Shaquille O'Neal, Chart 35 on page 122.

American athlete, author, actor, and rap artist. At 7 feet 1 inch tall and 303 pounds, he is the basketball superstar of the Los Angeles Lakers. As the biggest colossus in NBA's history, O'Neal's contract with the Los Angeles Lakers was the largest in the history of sports, signing on July 18, 1996 for seven years

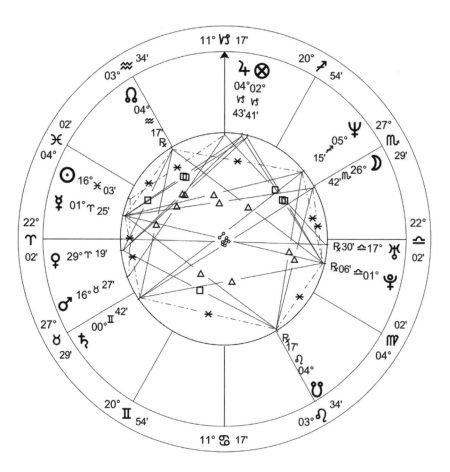

Chart 35. Ascendant conjunct Cardinal Axis: Shaquille O'Neal, March 6, 1972, 8:00 AM EST, Newark, NJ 40N49, 74W13.

at $120 million. O'Neal, also called "Shaq," "Superman," and "The Big Aristotle," is best known for his signature slam dunk, shattering backboards, and dashing the hopes of the opposing team. The only son of Lucille O'Neal and Joe Toney, Shaquille Raushaun O'Neal, whose first name means "Little Warrior" in Arabic, was abandoned at birth by Toney, leaving Lucille a single mom. In 1974 Lucille married ambitious coworker Philip Harrison, who joined the army that same year. Harrison had three children of his own and, with the addition of Lucille and Shaq to support he often worked three jobs to get a slice of the American Dream.

By age five O'Neal was so tall his mother had to carry his birth certificate to prove his age. Raised on army bases in the United States and West Germany, O'Neal was a rebellious child despite his stepfather's strict military discipline. At 13, the 6 foot 7 inch giant discovered basketball in West Germany, and his wayward days ended. Two years later, as a high school junior in San Antonio, Texas, O'Neal led the team to an undefeated season. The following year he led the team as an All-American to a state championship.

Attending Louisiana State University on an athletic scholarship, he was two-time All American, two-time Southeastern Conference player of the year, and national player of the year in 1991. He left LSU in his junior year in 1992 after being drafted by the Orlando Magic, spending the summer under the tutelage of Earvin "Magic" Johnson. His first season with Orlando in 1993 was so exceptional the NBA named him Rookie of the Year. In the summer of that same year O'Neal was featured in *Blue Chips*, a film about college recruits playing pro basketball, and recorded a rap music album *The Way It's Goin' Down*.

In O'Neal's second and third seasons with Orlando, he averaged 29 points per game and in 1994 led the NBA in scoring. After missing 28 games in the 1995–1996 season due to injuries, O'Neal was named to the United States Olympic Dream Team. At the Olympic Games in Atlanta, O'Neal's famous slam dunks helped the U.S. win the gold medal in men's basketball.

In 1996–1997 season O'Neal joined the Los Angeles Lakers under his unprecedented contract. By the 1999–2000 season he and Lakers' shooting guard Kobe Bryant made one of the most effective guard–center combinations in NBA history, despite their fractious personal relationship. Together they led the Los Angeles Lakers to three consecutive NBA titles in 2000, 2001 and 2002. With the highest scoring average for center in NBA finals history, O'Neal was voted the Most Valuable Player each year. In 2004 the Lakers offered him another contract under which he would have remained the highest paid player in the league, but only by a small margin. O'Neal refused and, after the Detroit Pistons defeated the Lakers in the 2004 NBA Finals, conflicts of interest with managers and coaches, including frequent public feuds with Bryant, led O'Neal to demand a trade. Joining the Miami Heat on July 14, 2004, O'Neal led the team to the best record in the Eastern Conference. The following year he signed a five-year extension with the Heat for $100 million dollars. On June 2, 2006, O'Neal, scoring 28 points, led the Miami Heat to the NBA finals for the first time in the teams' eighteen-year history.

In addition to his superstar status as an athlete, O'Neal has made several rap albums, including *Shaq Diesel* (1993), which sold over a million copies, *You Can't Stop the Reign* (1996), and *Respect* (1998). After O'Neal's natural father, Joe Toney, identified himself to O'Neal, he explicitly dismissed him in a rap song entitled "Biological Didn't Bother."

O'Neal giant dimensions are popular in video games including *NBA Jam*, *Shaq Fu* and *Ready 2 Rumble*. He has appeared in several film, notably *Blue Chips* (1997), *Kazaam* (1996), and *Good Burger* (1997).

Promising his mother he would complete his education, O'Neal graduated LSU with a bachelor's degree in business with a minor in political science on December 15, 2000 and received a master's degree in business on June 25, 2005. "Someday I might have to put down a basketball and have a regular nine-to-five like everybody else." Every Christmas he plays "Shaqa Claus," personally distributing free toys to children across the nation and on "Shaqsgiving" hands out free turkeys. With a strong need to help and protect, he graduated police academy and has been sworn in as an officer in Los Angeles and Miami. In March 2005 he was named national spokesperson for Safe Surfin', a foundation that tracks down sexual predators who target children on the internet, and plans to work with the special victims detective unit to stop crimes against children. Stating he does not seek "photo ops," he wants to "get down and dirty," and make arrests.

O'Neal married his long time girlfriend Shaunie Nelson on December 26, 2002 at the Beverly Hills Hotel. She is the mother of two of his children; he had two children from prior relationships and Shaunie had one. Their fourth child was born on May 1, 2006.

Shaquille O'Neal's Ascendant, conjunct the Cardinal Axis within 28 minutes, illustrates his extraordinary appearance and his resultant abilities to land him in the public eye. Both the Sun and Mars tie as Principal Planets, emphasizing physical prowess and protection (Mars) and his creativity and need to help children (the Sun). Mars, ruling O'Neal's Ascendant and thus his ruling planet, is also conjunct the Cardinal Axis with a wide orb of one degree and 28 minutes, further underscoring his high-profile personal presentation.

Chapter Six

IT RUNS IN THE FAMILY

*Tradition does not mean that the living are dead,
it means that the dead are living.*

HAROLD MACMILLAN

When one's public presentation and Midheaven are a representation of tradition or heredity, the Principal Planet takes a back seat to the Moon and Saturn, the familial signs of Cancer and Capricorn and the rulers of the MC and IC. The individual is "branded" with a powerful genetic code that will predispose them to walk in the footsteps of a parent or grandparent. They find their niche maintaining a family business or tradition, or as the carrier of an inherited talent, ability, congenital health condition, or illness with one or more of the horoscopic placements, listed in order of strength:

- The signs Cancer or Capricorn on the MC/IC axis
- Moon or Saturn in the 4th or 10th house or conjunct the MC/IC axis
- The ruler of the MC and/or IC is in the sign of Cancer or Capricorn

- Ruler of the MC/IC in the fourth or tenth house
- Rulers of the MC and IC are in Ptolemaic aspect
- Moon and Saturn in aspect

The above planetary placements serve as genetic markers of nothing less than raging genes that can seal one's fate for better or worse. Familial characteristics will manifest in individuals with these placements as neon lights and their position as hereditary torch-bearer or victim is their own personal two-edged sword. Whether progenitors or heirs, these crucial gene-bearing individuals are walking memory banks of DNA that can make or break their destinies. Often the impact of their ancestral influence, particularly health conditions, may not manifest until middle age. Once triggered, however, these shadowed genes will flicker on their twisted ladder and soon blaze as bright as the Las Vegas strip. Fortune turns its wheel.

The horoscope of Liza Minelli, Chart 36, provides an example of a chart with Cancer/Capricorn MC/IC axis.

American singer and actress, daughter of the immortal entertainer Judy Garland and Hollywood film director Vincente Minnelli, Liza Minnelli is part of a select group that has won an Academy Award, an Emmy, a Tony and a Grammy. She has the distinction of being one of the few Academy Award winners whose parents were both Academy Award *nominees,* and is the only winner of that award whose parents were also both *winners* of it. "My family goes back six generations in the theatre and the circus on both sides. I'm purebred show business. Mama taught me to plant my feet on the earth but keep my head in the sky."[1] She made her film debut at age three in the musical *In the Good Old Summertime,* and her stage debut at age 5 dancing to her mother singing "Swanee" at the New York Palace Theatre. That same year her parents divorced. At 13 she was featured on a Gene Kelly television special and by 1961 was touring Europe in her high school production in the title role of Anne Frank. In 1965, she launched her musical career with her mother at Garland's sensational concert at the London Pal-

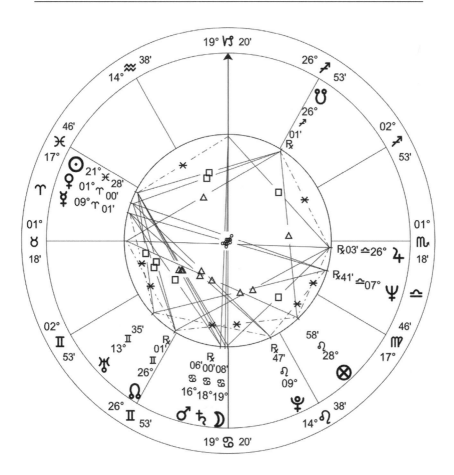

Chart 36. Cancer/Capricorn MC/IC axis: Liza Minelli, March 12, 1946, 7:58 AM PST Los Angeles, CA 34N04 118W15.

ladium, taking the audience by storm and, according to many reviews, even upstaging Garland herself. A sense of competition ensued between mother and daughter, putting the already unstable Garland more on edge. "I was on stage with my mother, but suddenly, she wasn't Mama... she was Judy Garland."[2]

Minnelli debuted on Broadway in 1965 in *Flora, the Red Menace*, winning a Tony for her performance. In 1967 her television special, "Liza with a Z," won her the Emmy. That same year her outstanding performance as Sally Bowles in the blockbuster film *Cabaret*, won her the Academy Award for Best Actress. Three years later her compelling vocal style was featured in the 1977 film *New York, New York*, where she earned her signature song, "New York, New York." In the 1980s and 1990s Minnelli won international acclaim for her live revues, including performances with Frank Sinatra and his new-fashioned Rat Pack. The pear didn't fall far from the tree. In the identical style of her mother, Minnelli projects an extremely needy and fragile persona whose booming alto voice brings the house down.

The family legacy runs deeper than over-the-top artistic talent. Minnelli's roller-coaster life has mirrored her mother's in more ways than one. Alcohol and drug addiction landed her in the Betty Ford clinic in 1984, the first of many rehabilitation attempts. Extreme weight fluctuation coupled with multiple surgeries to replace both hips, both knees, three crushed discs, rotated vertebrae, and spinal fusion only increased her dependency on drugs. Treatment of a suspected heart attack in 2000 revealed viral encephalitis, an illness that almost took her life. When faced with the prospect of spending her life in a wheelchair, Minnelli consoled herself with food and drink, requiring a return to rehab to regain her mental, spiritual, and physical health. After a strict diet and dancing three hours a day she lost sixty-five pounds and is still losing. Four marriages, four divorces, and three miscarriages have taken a serious toll, sending the deeply troubled Minnelli into psychiatric treatment and continuous legal disputes. "If you had cancer you go back for treatment, wouldn't you? ....We all help each other and the support is amazing...families are put back together...things which weren't available when I was dealing with my mom. There's no cure for alcoholism. The only thing that helps you is your attitude. Mama was chemically dependent and an alcoholic, so was her father, and now we know that it is a compulsive, inherited disease."[3]

After years of setbacks, Minnelli returned to the New York stage in 2002 in a show-stopping performance that was hailed as nothing less than "a resurrection."[4]

Cancer and Capricorn on Minnelli's MC/IC axis with the Moon conjunct her IC underscore her neon genes that would predispose her family legacy to mark her life in an unmistakable manner for better or worse. She has lived out her lineal blueprint as being almost a clone of her mother in both public and private life. Genes don't lie.

• • •

Chart 37 on page 132, the horoscope of Steve Forbes, provides an example of Saturn in the 4th as carrier of tradition.

American publisher, journalist, author, CEO of *Forbes*, and U. S. Republican candidate for President in 1996 and 2000, Steve Forbes is the son of entrepreneur Malcolm Stevenson Forbes, the founder of *Forbes Capitalist Tool*, the leading business magazine in America. After the death of his illustrious father in 1990, Forbes assumed his father's role of editor-in-chief. He significantly expanded readership worldwide by adding *Forbes Life*, *Forbes Asia*, the *Gilder Technology Report* and by publishing *Forbes Magazine* in Chinese, Korean, Japanese, Russian, Arabic, Hebrew, and Polish. With a circulation of over 900,000, the combined total of Forbes publications, encompassing over ten magazines and fourteen newspapers, reaches a global audience of over five million readers. Forbes is the only writer to have won the prestigious Crystal Owl Award four times, the prize given to the financial journalist whose economic forecasts for the coming year proved most accurate. His editorials appear in each edition of Forbes under "Fact and Comment."

Thanks to Malcolm senior's notoriety as a wealthy libertine, Forbes enjoyed a privileged childhood on his father's estate. His interest in politics showed early, staging mock conventions with his stuffed animals. After graduating the Brooks boarding school in North Andover, Massachusetts in 1966, he entered Princeton University where in 1968 he continued the family legacy by launching a campus business magazine with two colleagues called *Business Today*. In 2006, Business Today. com was the website of the largest student-run publication in

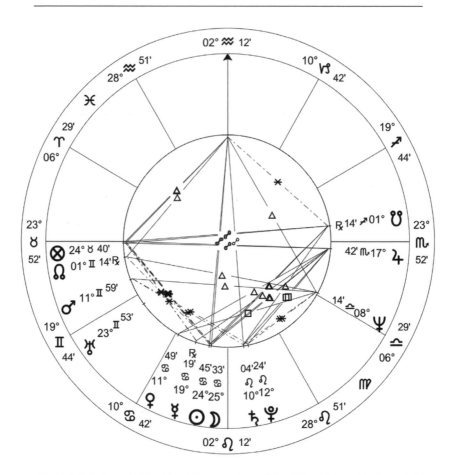

Chart 37. Saturn in the Fourth as carrier of tradition: Steve Forbes, July 18 1947, 1:35 AM EDT, Morristown, NJ 40N47, 74W28.

America. Upon graduation from Princeton in 1968, Forbes declined to enlist for Vietnam, thinking the war was "a mistake." After six years of service in the Coast Guard, he joined the family magazine business in 1974 and by 1982 was deputy editor-in-chief. Following the death of his father in 1990, Forbes assumed total control of the publishing empire initially established by his grandfather Bertram Charles Forbes. His brothers Christopher Forbes, vice-chairman, Robert Forbes, and Timothy Forbes have all worked for the family business,

132

but Father Malcom left 51% of the voting shares to son Steve, clearly establishing him as the leader.

With the international influence of the family publications, Forbes was appointed as chairman of the board for International Broadcasting from 1985–1993, supervising the operations of Radio Free Europe and Radio Liberty. Working behind the Iron Curtain, Forbes' broadcasts were praised by Polish Solidarity leader Lech Walesa as being crucial in Poland's movement in breaking free from communism.

On September 22, 1995 Forbes announced he would run for the Republican nomination for president. Accepting no federal funds whatsoever he financed his entire campaign with his own fortune. The highlights of his platform included replacing the seventeen million word federal tax code with a flat 17 percent income tax, medical savings accounts, free trade, downsizing government agencies to balance the budget, opposing gun control, pollution control, and opposing the legalization of drugs. Falling far short of winning the Republican nomination in 1996 and 2000, he returned to his position of chair of the magazine and Forbes, Inc.

Forbes is the author of *A New Birth of Freedom* in 1999 and *The Flat Tax Revolution: Using a Postcard to Abolish the IRS* in 2005. He married Sabina Beekman in 1971 and is the father of five daughters. He appears as a frequent panelist on his television news program "Forbes on Fox" on the Fox News Channel.

Forbes' Saturn in the 4th house points to carrying on a family tradition. With Saturn ruling his 9th house, media and publishing are key components in facilitating his legacy. Saturn coruling his 10th and 11th houses (using the Placidus house system), further emphasizes technology (Aquarius) and groups (11th house) of investors across the globe.

● ● ●

The horoscope of Alexandra, Czarina of Russia, Chart 38 on page 134, provides an example of MC/IC ruler in Cancer or Capricorn as carrier of a genetic health condition.

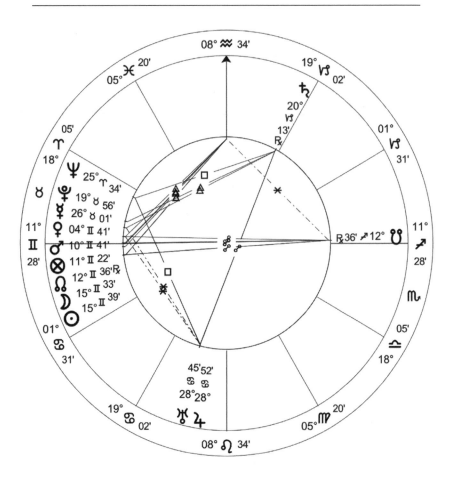

Chart 38. MC/IC Ruler in Cancer or Capricorn as carrier of a genetic health condition: Alexandra, Czarina of Russia, June 6, 1872, 3:45 AM LMT, Darmstadt, Germany 49N53, 8E40.

This German princess, who was empress consort of the Russian Empire and the wife of Nicholas II of Russia, carried the hemophilia gene into the royal Romanov family, resulting in her son, the Czarevich Nikolai, being born a hemophiliac. His illness affected the fate of a nation.

Princess Alix Victoria Helena Louise Beatrice of Hesse was the granddaughter of Queen Victoria and the fifth of seven children of Prince Louis IV of Hesse Darmstadt and Princess Alice.

Her lighthearted personality earned her the nickname "Sunny," but after the death of her mother at age six, Sunny became morose and withdrawn and, due to declining family finances, spent years with Queen Victoria as her rumored favorite granddaughter at Balmoral and the Isle of Wight. Alix proved a precocious student and an excellent pianist, but extreme self-consciousness left her doing needlepoint and listening to Wagner.

Following her marriage to her beloved distant cousin Czarevich Nicholas of Russia on November 26, 1894, Alix changed her name to Alexandra Feodorovna, converted to the Orthodox Church, and had four daughters in rapid succession. Despite having intelligence, talent, and multilingual expertise, she lacked social skills and was not popular at court or with the Russian people, who were disappointed that she did not produce an heir to the throne. Finally, on August 12, 1904, she gave birth to a son Alexei, and all of Russia rejoiced. It was to be a brief revelry. Two months later Alexei was diagnosed with hemophilia, an incurable and often fatal disease at that time. With her most important role of bearing a male child being fulfilled, Alexandra completely withdrew from public life and focused on Alexei's delicate condition. The best physicians in Russia and Europe were called in, but all treatments proved futile except the one used by the monk Rasputin. Prayer. Rasputin was a mystic and gifted faith healer, and became Alexandra's chief resource to protect her son. But gossip spread, and the Czar separated him from his family. After a near-death hemorrhage for Alexei, however, the distraught Alexandra sent a telegram to the holy man. Rasputin's returned telegram, confirming that Alexei would not die, inexplicably arrived at the moment of Alexei's awakening. Thus the die was cast. Alexandra's made Rasputin a permanent presence in the royal family to relieve any of Alexei's potential suffering.

Czar Nicholas was singularly unsuited to ruling an empire that encompassed one-sixth of the earth and, after leaving Alexandra as the de facto ruler in his absence during World War I, it became apparent that she was even less suited to the task. Under

Rasputin's advice, her continuous and flippant removal and reappointment of ministers resulted in a dangerously unstable government. Germany, Russia's enemy during the war, soundly defeated Russian armies in several battles and, since Alexandra was of German origin, rumor spread that she was a German spy. Her popularity plummeted and the nation gradually unraveled. Despite complaints from both public and private sectors, the absentee Czar Nicholas defended his wife against all odds.

A naive and autocratic ruler, Czar Nicholas, firmly believing in the divine right of kings, was never in touch with the general population. By January 1917, the capital city of St. Petersburg had no electricity, running water, or newspapers. Fuel shortages prevented rail shipment of food and supplies to both soldiers and civilians. When Czar Nicholas was advised to "break down the barrier that separates you from your people to regain their confidence,"[5] he ignored the recommendation. Rampant inflation and food shortages provoked strikes and public protest. The Russian Revolution began the following month, and on March 15, 1917 (N.S.) Nicholas abdicated his throne.

Alexandra, her husband, and children were exiled to Yekaterinburg and held captive. They were executed by firing squad on the night of July 17, 1918. On August 14, 2000, the Russian Orthodox Church canonized her and her family.

Saturn, the coruler of Alexandra's MC, is retrograde in Capricorn, indicating the passing on of a genetic trait. Her Principal Planet is Mars, coruling her 6th house of illness and ruling her 12th house of seclusion. Alexandra withdrew from public life (12th house) and spent most of her time as a nurse (6th house) to her son's illness, which was kept a secret (12th house) from the nation and even from certain members of the Romanov household. Her intractable penchant for privacy (12th house) and alliance with Rasputin caused scandal (12th house), which led to her self-undoing (12th house) and further undermined her reputation with the Russian people.

Chapter 7

ROYAL FIXED STARS

*The Fixed Stars give great gifts and elevate even
from poverty to an extreme height of Fortune,
the Seven Planets do not so.*[1]

WILLIAM LILLY

Since prehistoric times, humankind has attempted to fathom
its earthly experience. Their first gesture toward this understanding may well have been a cave dweller lifting his or her
eyes toward the heavens in wonder and speculation of forth-
coming events. The sky could tell stories, it held omens. It fore-
told weather conditions, which in turn affected travel, hunting, and agriculture. Daylight and darkness were measured by
the rise and fall of those two majestic objects, the Sun and the
Moon. The ancients used the sky as their blueprint for action.
The so-called "Wise People" were those who made a thorough
study of the patterns of planets and stars, and observed how to
use them as signposts. Observations were made regarding how
Mother Nature mirrored events in the heavens. Shellfish activity and the rhythms of the tides coincided with phases of the
moon. Seafaring peoples, lacking compasses, used the North

Star and constellations for navigation. The Egyptians repeatedly observed that the Nile flooded every time the star Sirius rose with the Sun. The clockwork that the ancients observed in the sky shaped and defined their annual calendars. Moreover, this time-honored system of celestial phenomena worked with a system.[2]

While attending their flocks, the ancient shepherds noticed regularity in the vast network of celestial display and handed down their observations in the oral tradition. Some bright stars stood still and some, which they referred to as "goat stars," wandered, just as their goats did. They noticed that more female sheep were born when goat stars were in certain places in the sky, and more male sheep were born when the goat stars were in other parts of the sky. Some stars twinkled, and others, mostly the goat stars, shone with a steady light. The Greeks named their goat stars *planetai*, meaning "wanderers." We call them planets. The bright, twinkling stars remained in a fixed position for hundreds of years. Thus they became known as the Fixed Stars. Their constancy proved invaluable for navigation and weather prediction. Four of these Fixed Stars held special status in the ancient world, for they marked the Four Pillars of Heaven. In the third century B.C.E. the ancient Sumerians used these Pillars of Heaven to mark the equinoxes and solstices, confirming the change of seasons by the Sun's transit in front of them. They are now commonly known as the Royal Fixed Stars:

- Aldebaran, at 9 degrees of Gemini at the spring equinox, the Eye of the Bull
- Regulus, at 29 degrees of Leo at the summer solstice, Cor Leonis or the Heart of the Lion. At this time of year the Sun shone at its strongest
- Antares, at 9 degrees Sagittarius, at the autumn equinox, the Heart of the Scorpion
- Formalhaut, at 3 degrees of Pisces, at the winter solstice, is the Fishes' Mouth

Note that the four ancient solstice points do not coincide with the modern solstice points discussed in Chapter 4. The earth's tilt over the millennia has changed the position of the solstice points. This continuous shift is known as the Precession of the Equinoxes, a shift that occurs when the equinoxes move through the sidereal zodiac as a result of the slow revolution of the earth's axis of rotation around the ecliptic pole.

Thus these Royal Fixed Stars functioned as the Cardinal Axis in the ancient world, and their degrees are just as powerful as the Cardinal Axis, perhaps even more so. They stay put, for we now know that they move only fifty seconds of motion per century. Similar to the Cardinal Axis, they give headline attention whether the individual seeks it or not. A Midheaven, Midheaven Ruler, or Principal Planet conjunct a Royal Fixed Star can be both a blessing and a curse. They impart extreme good fortune but the native must live the spotlight. Like gifted and talented kids, they're plucked from the crowd and placed in the public eye to their great advantage, receiving helping hands along the way as they seemingly float up to the top. But life is not all a bed of roses. Like members of a royal family, their privacy is limited, and their mistakes are Big Mistakes that are open for public scrutiny and criticism. While Royal Fixed Stars do not imply happiness or contentment, they do portend high recognition and notoriety. Royalty, like everything else, has its price, and their bill is paid in the front-page news. When one is up so high, the only place to go is down.

• • •

Chart 39 on page 140, the horoscope of Jay Leno, provides an example of Midheaven conjunct a Royal Fixed Star.

Jay Leno is the American comedian who replaced Johnny Carson as talk show host of the *Tonight Show*, the second longest running entertainment program in U. S. history. Known for regularly delivering the longest monologue of any late night show, Leno boasts an estimated 5.7 million viewers per evening.

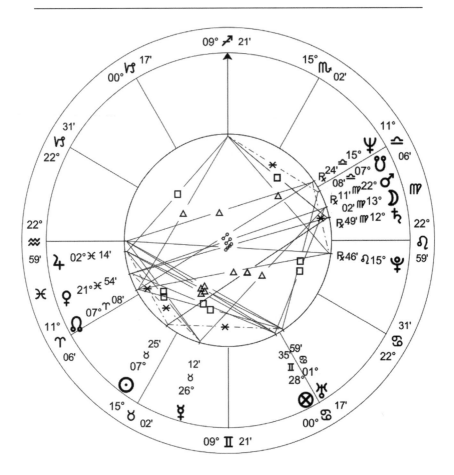

Chart 39. Midheaven conjunct a Royal Fixed Star: Jay Leno, April 28, 1950, 2:03 AM EST New Rochelle, NY 40N54, 73W46.

James Douglas Muir Leno is the youngest of two sons of Scottish born Catherine Muir and insurance salesman Angelo Leno. Growing up in Andover, Massachusetts, the dyslexic Leno was an indifferent student, but excelled at being the class clown, causing his fifth-grade teacher to comment, "If Jay spent as much time studying as he does trying to be a comedian, he'd be a big star." Finding humor to be his salvation, young Leno followed the careers of comedians including Alan King, Rodney Dangerfield, and Robert Klein.

While attending Emerson College in Boston majoring in speech, he worked the open mike and comedy club circuit. After graduation in 1973, Leno moved to Los Angeles to pursue a comedy career in Hollywood, seeking work at NBC studios in Burbank. He found work as a comedy writer for the TV sitcom *Good Times*, and landed bit parts in films *Fun With Dick and Jane* (1977), *American Hot Wax* (1978), *Silver Bears* (1978) and *Americathon* (1979). For much of the late '70s and '80s, Leno often worked three hundred nights a year on the comedy club circuit honing his skills as a stand-up, interspersed with appearances on game shows and TV commercials. Word reached Johnny Carson to have the big-chinned, avuncular comic appear on his show. Carson saw Leno's act but declined to sign him on, telling Leno his material couldn't hold his audience's attention. Actor Steve Martin forced the issue and, in 1977, Carson introduced Leno to millions of viewers on his show. He returned thirty-eight times before replacing Carson as the host of the *Tonight Show* on May 25, 1992. Leno is known for avoiding vulgarity in his jokes to accommodate the mainstream.

A lifelong antique car and motorcycle enthusiast, Leno writes a column for *Popular Mechanics Magazine* and is a member of the National Advisory Board of McPherson College, the only accredited college with a degree in auto restoration. In 2001 he auctioned off one of his Harley-Davidson motorcycles to aid victims of September 11th, and did so again for the 2004 Indian Ocean earthquake and in 2005 for Hurricane Katrina.

Leno married Mavis Nichols in 1980. They live in Beverly Hills where Leno maintains his car and motorcycle collection and Mavis displays her antiques. Feminist Mavis Leno is an activist to end the abuse of women under Taliban rule.

Leno's MC conjunct Royal Fixed Star Antares at 9 degrees Sagittarius serves as an indicator of being selected and placed in the public eye of outstanding success. After years of hard work and help from fellow entertainers, he surpassed all competition and was awarded the coveted position as host of the *Tonight Show*.

• • •

The horoscope of Sybil Leek, Chart 40, provides an example of Midheaven ruler conjunct a Royal Fixed Star.

British witch, psychic, astrologer, author, and activist, Sybil Leek has been dubbed "Britain's most famous witch." She is the author of over sixty books on occult practices, and has promoted Wicca into public consciousness in the twentieth century. Born into English gentry of Irish and Russian descent, she was raised in Hampshire in an unorthodox family whose members were skilled in esoteric traditions. Attending school for only three years, her father, mother, and grandmother taught her at home, with each instructing her in their own area of interest. Her mother was a psychic, her father a naturalist who studied Eastern philosophies, and her grandmother was a witch and professional astrologer, whose clients included H.G. Wells, who showed little Sybil her first eclipse, Thomas Hardy, and T. E. Lawrence (Lawrence of Arabia). Sybil demonstrated a talent for writing in her early childhood and one family friend, Aleister Crowley, encouraged her to write poetry. The members of her mother's eclectic tea parties were called "The Pentagram Club."

The Leek family were very proud of their heritage. Sybil could trace her mother's ancestry to witches in Ireland in 1185 and, on her father's side, to occultists who practiced for royalty in czarist Russia. One notable ancestor was unmarried Molly Leigh, born in 1685, who earned a living selling milk from her own herd and kept a jackdaw perched on her shoulder as a familiar. Customers and townspeople grew suspicious of her solitary self-reliance and blamed her for local problems and ailments, culminating in an accusation of witchcraft. Molly sidestepped persecution and died of natural causes in 1746, but many claim her ghost still haunts the churchyard.

The well-heeled Leeks vacationed in the French Riviera and, during one sojourn there, in a ceremony arranged by her grandmother, 15-year-old Sybil was initiated into a coven to replace her aunt as High Priestess. Entering a conservatory in the fall

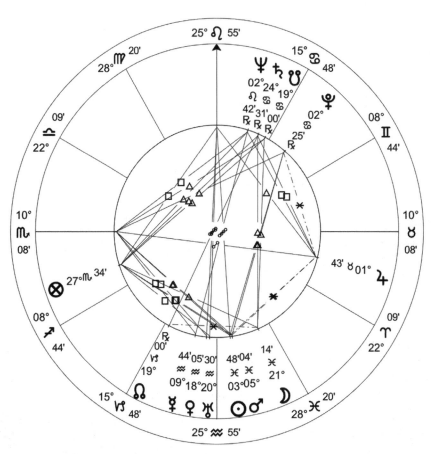

Chart 40. Midheaven Ruler conjunct a Royal Fixed Star: Sybil Leek, February 22, 1917, 11:52 PM , GMT Staffordshire, England.

of that same year, Sybil fell in love with a well-known pianist twenty-four years her senior, whose name she never disclosed, and the couple eloped soon after her 16th birthday. They toured England and Europe but tragedy struck when her husband died suddenly two years later. Widowed and desolate, Sybil returned to live with her beloved grandmother.

At the outbreak of World War II, Sybil joined the Red Cross, working as nurse in military hospitals in London, the Hebrides, and on Anzio beach in Italy. The culture shock was absolute. She and her team of young society women were transformed into

> hardened Boadiceas, ready to be in the thick of battle 24 hours day...we had forgotten what the word "lady" meant...When people knew I was an astrologer, they would come to ask what the stars foretold. Nearly everyone getting his orders for active duty came to me and we tried to laugh about charts, fortune telling and psychic phenomenon. Many men had an intuitive feeling that they would never come back, and it was a sad time to be doing horoscopes—a far cry from the glorious days of the Riviera. No one had much money and fees were never mentioned.[3]

After the war Sybil returned to Hampshire, living with her family on the edge of the New Forest, where Sybil lived for a year with Romany Gypsies, learning their traditions and increasing her knowledge of herbs. Adopting her as one of their own who followed the "old ways," the gypsies honored her with the title of "The Lady." During this time she attended rituals with the Horsa coven of the New Forest, which had allegedly practiced in secret since the twelfth century.

Returning to mundane life in her late twenties, Sybil opened an antique shop in the village of Burley, publicly practicing witchcraft after the Witchcraft Laws were repealed in 1951. After publishing articles and appearing regularly on BBC radio and television, the resulting outcry of controversy forced her out of her shop, with her landlord demanding that she renounce witchcraft or lose her lease. There was no turning back.

Sybil, now married with two young sons, emigrated to America where she launched a writing career, publishing a series of books including the bestsellers *Diary of a Witch* (1968), and *My Life In Astrology* (1974). Her work is often cited as the first user-friendly presentation of witchcraft as a religion and a system of spiritual belief. Her magazine, *Sybil Leek's Astrol-*

ogy, informed readers that astrology was based on mathematics and was more scientific than Sun Sign columns. In a nod to her ancestor Molly Leigh, she often appeared in public with her pet jackdaw, Mr. Hotfoot Jackson, perched on her shoulder.

She died in Melbourne, Florida, on October 26, 1982, of cancer.

The Sun, ruler of Sybil's Midheaven, is exactly conjunct Royal Fixed Star Formalhaut at 3 degrees Pisces, and points to her being singled out and given preferential treatment. Note the position of the Moon in the fourth house as indicative of one carried on a tradition and whose hereditary characteristics were manifested in her public presentation.

• • •

F. Scott Fitzgerald, Chart 41 on page 146, provides an example of Principal Planet conjunct a Royal Fixed Star.

American novelist, short story author, and screenwriter who depicted, chronicled, and personified the Jazz Age, Fitzgerald is perhaps best known for his masterpiece, *The Great Gatsby,* considered the Great American Novel, and a standard text in high schools and universities worldwide.

Francis Scott Key Fitzgerald, named after the author of *The Star Spangled Banner* (who was his cousin three times removed), was the only son of Edward, an unsuccessful furniture sales- man, and Mary (Mollie) McQuillan, daughter of a wealthy St. Paul grocer. The family lived in Buffalo, New York until 1908 when, after Edward was fired from his job, they moved back to St. Paul where they lived comfortably on Mollie's inheritance. Fitzgerald's writing ability was evident in youth; at 13 his first story appeared in the school newspaper. From 1911–1913 he attended a Catholic prep school in New Jersey, where a priest encouraged his literary ambitions. Accepted to Princeton Uni- versity in 1913, Fitzgerald neglected his studies while he wrote scripts and lyrics for the Princeton Triangle Club musicals, con- tributed to *The Tiger* humor magazine and the Nassau Literary Magazine. He fell in love with socialite Ginevra King, who later

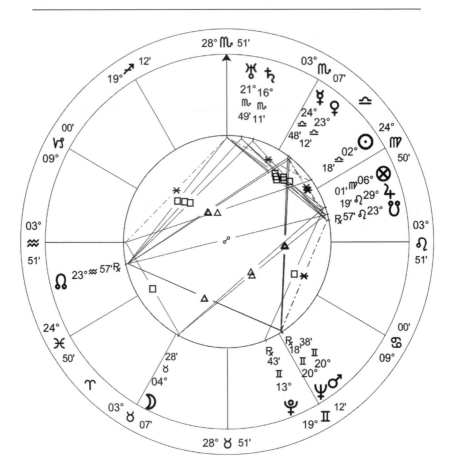

Chart 41. Principal Planet conjunct a Royal Fixed Star: F. Scott Fitzgerald, September 24, 1896, 3:30 PM LMT St. Paul, MN 44N46, 93W05.

served as the prototype for Daisy Buchanan, and mingled with the sons of wealthy families from the Eastern seaboard over whose extravagant parties he would obsess for the rest of his life. With graduation unlikely after being placed on academic probation in his senior year, Scott joined the army in 1917, commissioned as a second lieutenant in the infantry. Believing he would die in combat, Fitzgerald promptly penned a novel, *The Romantic Egoist*. Its rejection letter praised the novel's originality, encouraging revision and resubmission.

146

Then came the watershed. In June 1918, Fitzgerald was stationed in Camp Sheridan in Montgomery, Alabama, where he fell in love with Zelda Sayre, the spoiled daughter of an Alabama Supreme Court judge and the "top girl," in his own words, of fashionable society. Their romance fueled Fitzgerald's revision of his novel, but it was rejected a second time. The war ended just as Fitzgerald was to be sent overseas and, needing to earn a living, he moved to New York City to write advertising copy and establish himself in order to marry. Impatient with Fitzgerald's plan and disinclined to live on his meager salary, Zelda broke the engagement.

Undaunted, Fitzgerald moved back to St. Paul where he rewrote his novel into *This Side of Paradise*. Published on March 26, 1920, *This Side of Paradise* was a bestseller, making 24 year old Fitzgerald an overnight sensation with assured financial success. Three weeks later on April 19, 1920, the couple married in New York at St. Patrick's Cathedral. Moving to Westport, Connecticut, they celebrated their success as they embarked on a rampageous lifestyle of continuous partying, madcap antics, and heavy drinking at the exquisite lawn parties of elitists. Fitzgerald, who wrote in one of his short stories "the rich are different from you and me,"[4] embraced and emulated their privileged world. The young couple moved to New York City where Fitzgerald wrote his second novel, *The Beautiful and the Damned,* then followed fellow artists and writers to France in 1921 where Fitzgerald befriended expatriate James Joyce who said "that young man must be mad—I'm afraid he'll do himself some injury."[5] After returning to St. Paul for the birth of their only child, Frances Scott Key ("Scottie") Fitzgerald on October 26, 1921, the undomesticated Fitzgeralds returned to the New York party circuit, then moved to France in 1924 where Fitzgerald cultivated friendships with Gertrude Stein and Ernest Hemingway. In 1925 he published *The Great Gatsby* to critical acclaim, yet the book did not provide the income Fitzgerald needed to support his indulgent lifestyle, requiring him to continuously write short stories that provided a high income from

American mainstream magazines. The couple epitomized Jazz Age expatriates in the European jet set for five years.

In the early 1930s Zelda was committed to sanitariums due to her deteriorating mental health. Obsessing over his wife's instability, Fitzgerald, an excessive drinker since college, descended into alcoholism. His novel *Tender Is the Night,* published in 1934, is about a psychiatrist's relationship with a mental patient. In 1935 he placed his daughter in boarding schools and no longer provided a home for her, making his agent her surrogate father but remaining her pen pal. Deeply in debt due to Zelda's medical care and his overall inability to manage finances, Fitzgerald moved to Hollywood in 1937 to write screenplays but was fired the following year because of his drinking. In a letter to his daughter he wrote "what I am doing here is the last tired effort of a man who once did something finer and better."[6]

Zelda, diagnosed with schizophrenia, was permanently placed in an institution. Fitzgerald, now estranged from her, began a relationship with gossip columnist Sheilah Graham. In 1939 he began another novel, *The Last Tycoon,* but ruined health had taken its toll, and he believed himself to be a failure as a writer. He died of a heart attack in Hollywood on December 21, 1940, before the book was finished. His work was revived in the middle 1950s and by 1960 he achieved a permanent place among America's best writers.

Jupiter, Fitzgerald's Principal Planet at 29 degrees Leo, works double duty as the Principal Planet conjunct a Royal Fixed Star. Catapulted into the limelight as a best-selling author at age 23, he was predisposed to associate with the privileged class, and chronicled the rich and famous on two continents while serving as a royal ambassador of the Jazz Age.

His extravagance ruined his health and left him in debt, sending him to an early death that left him unable to reap his literary legacy of universal appeal. When critics chided his continuous preoccupation with romance and high living he replied, "But my God, it was my material, and it was all I had to deal with."[7]

Another Fixed Star used in the Slevin System is Spica, "The Virgin's Spike," at 23 degrees Libra. While this Fixed Star is not royal and did not mark solstice or equinox points in ancient times, it still bestows preferential treatment, giving recognition, good fortune and, above all, protection, a commodity the Royal Stars do not accord. If the person makes mistake it will still become public knowledge, and falls from grace may generate a deafening sound. But in the end, despite the outcome, the person is offered veneration and protection, with accolades abounding.

• • •

The horoscope of Diana, Princess of Wales, shown as Chart 42 on page 150, provides an example of Spica conjunct the Midheaven.

British royalty, daughter of the 8th Earl of Spencer, with lineage dating back to fifteenth century, Diana was known as "The People's Princess." She gained international recognition through her marriage to Prince Charles on July 29, 1981.

Diana was the youngest daughter of Edward John Spencer and his first wife Frances Burke Roche, with two older sisters and two brothers, one older and one younger. At her parents' separation, the mother took the two youngest children to live in London but lost custody of them in a particularly fractious divorce. Upon her father inheriting the title of 8th Earl Spencer, she became Lady Diana and was raised by a nanny in her family's ancestral home of Althorp. Unable to complete secondary school due to poor academic performance, she attended a finishing school in Switzerland then moved to London at 16 where she worked at a nursery school, showing a natural aptitude for children. Of royal descent dating back to the Stuarts and, as a member of the Church of England and an aristocratic virgin without a past, she fit the bill as a potential bride for Prince Charles, who was her personal idol. With sumptuous regalia, the couple married in St. Paul's Cathedral in London on July 29, 1981 at a televised royal wedding viewed by a global audience

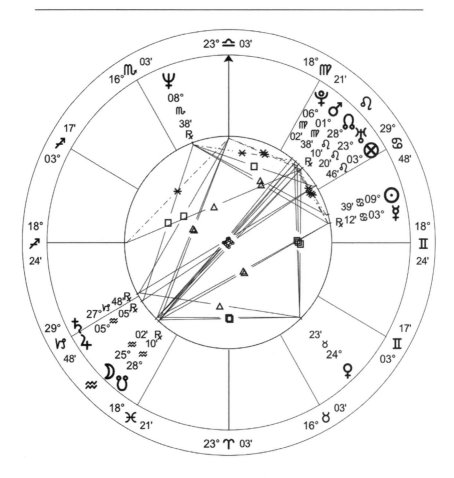

Chart 42. Spica conjunct the Midheaven: Diana, Princess of Wales, July 1, 1961, 7:45 PM BST, Sandringham, England. 52N50, 0E30.

of almost one billion. For the proverbial better or worse, her marriage transformed her status into one of the richest, most glamorous, and socially powerful women in the world. With wholesome beauty as fresh and clean as the English countryside, her guileless, unassuming manner gave her a unique appeal that endeared her to the masses. Her common touch was palpable; Diana held the hands of dying AIDS patients, attended land-mine victims, the handicapped, and the homeless. She possessed an instinctive compassion that reached into the hearts of the needy, resulting in a meteoric popularity that eclipsed her husband and his family. As a fashion icon, charity worker, and world-class celebrity, members of the royal family disliked her for appearing more as a pop diva in public than as a proper princess in the palace. And the strain showed.

The fairy tale marriage showed its dark side from the beginning. Prince Charles resumed his relationship with his former paramour, Camilla Parker Bowles. Rejected and betrayed, Diana, bulimic and emotionally fragile, began a series of ill-fated affairs that she later made public in televised interviews. Her lack of discretion in blending her private life with her public persona shocked the royal family, who kept her at arm's length. Diana later deeply regretted her public declarations and interviews.

After the birth of her two sons, Prince William on June 21, 1982 and Prince Harry on September 15, 1984, she found her niche in motherhood, yet the royal family criticized her for displaying her devotion and spending so much time with them. Embracing the fashion culture, Diana was indisputably one of the best-dressed women in the world and, to her deep distress, certainly the most photographed. Whether training at a gym, playing with her sons or Trooping the Color, Diana's persona was open season for the paparazzi, who hunted her like a big-game animal. The media, particularly the British tabloids, scrutinized her relentlessly, resulting in Diana's life lived as a serial melodrama performed in the public eye, with every plot twist and nuance broadcasted to a world audience. Manipulating the press to project her compelling image as the betrayed spouse and the radiant socialite, Diana shocked and dismayed the Royal family, who found her behavior inappropriate and were not amused. Despite a damaged reputation through her belatedly regretted public confessions, her public appeal never waned. Viewing her marriage as a sham, Diana and Charles separated on December 9, 1992, and finally divorced on August 28, 1996. She was still a member of the Royal Family, as she was the mother of the second and third in line to the throne, and maintained a home in Kensington Palace.

With her sons in boarding school, Diana, now a free agent, further embraced charity work and pursued her own interests in music, fashion, travel, and consulting New Age practitioners.

She died tragically on August 31, 1997, after a high-speed car accident in Paris with her paramour Dodi Al-Fayed. The public outpouring of grief was overwhelming; over 2 billion people worldwide watched her televised funeral.

Princess Diana's Midheaven is exactly conjunct Spica, indicating her rank or public presentation was marked with extreme good fortune. With the Midheaven also serving as the family axis, as it is the point opposite the IC, or family foundation, Diana had a royal pedigree dating back to the sixteenth century. Protection came in the virtual network of royal security and trusted bodyguards, one of whom, Ken Wharfe, immortalized Diana in his book *Diana: Closely Guarded Secret*, and Trevor Reese-Jones, who survived the fatal car accident.

• • •

An example of Midheaven Ruler conjunct Spica is shown in Chart 43, the horoscope of Roy Horn.

German-American magician and entertainer, Roy Horn is half of the magic and illusion act "Siegfried and Roy," which became renowned internationally for the big cats included in their act, in particular white tigers but also white lions as well.

Uwe Ludwig Horn was born during a World War II bombing, prior to which his mother, Johanna, rode a bicycle to her sister's home in order to give birth. At the time of Roy's birth, his father was in a Russian POW camp, returning to his family as an unstable alcoholic. Divorcing at the end of the war, Johanna's second husband was also an alcoholic, sending Roy, the youngest of four brothers, to seek companionship with his half-wolf dog that he named Hexe, the German word for "witch," or someone who could work magic. The two were inseparable. Once when they were walking in the woods, Roy strayed into a patch of reeds while following a raven, and found he was sinking in quicksand. Hexe, sensing his master's

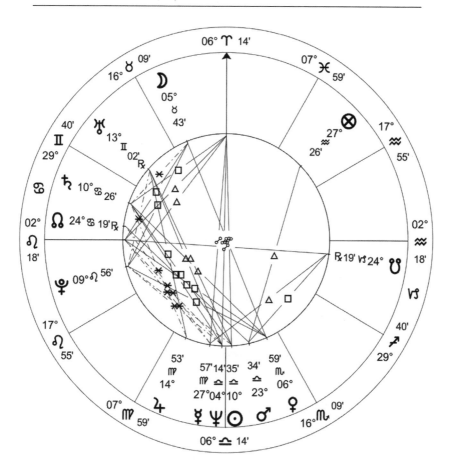

Chart 43. Midheaven Ruler conjunct Spica: Roy Horn, October 3, 1944, 11:57 PM MET Nordenham, Germany, 53N29, 8E28.

panic, sprinted away, returning quickly with a farmer to save young Roy from certain death. The experience left Roy indelibly imprinted with the trust that could prevail between humans and animals. Finding solace from his unpleasant home life in the Bremen Zoo, he developed a deep rapport through the bars of a cage with a two-year-old cheetah named Chico, earning the animal's complete trust. The zoo workers eventually gave Roy permission to enter Chico's cage, feed him, and even take him for walks. Thus began Roy's bonding to big cats.

At age 13, Roy ran away from home. He found employment on a cruise ship and smuggled his beloved Chico on board, liberating him from the zoo. After hearing the applause of a stage act one night, Roy saw 18 year old Siegfried (Siegfried Fischbacher), a magician, pull a rabbit out of a hat. The two young boys began an instant friendship, and Roy soon became Siegfried's assistant. When Siegfried asked Roy what he thought of his magic, Roy replied that it was too predictable, stating "If you can make a rabbit and dove disappear, can you do the same with a cheetah?" Siegfried responded, "In magic, anything is possible."[8] So the act developed into their trademark magic with big cats. Siegfried and Roy spent the next five years performing through Europe with little to moderate success. A performance at the casino in Monte Carlo brought an invitation to Las Vegas where Siegfried and Roy opened in 1967. Their popularity soared. By 1972 they received the Las Vegas Entertainment Award for Best Show of the Year and in 1974 they opened at the MGM Grand. Two years later the American Academy of Magical Arts named them Magicians of the Year. In 1989 their performance run at Radio City Music Hall broke a 57-year box office record. The following year they opened at the Las Vegas Mirage Hotel for an annual guarantee of $57.5 million, signing a lifetime contract in 2000. That same year they were honored as the Magicians of the Century.

Disaster struck on Roy's 59th birthday on October 3, 2003, when one of his beloved white tigers, which he had raised since birth, mauled him during a show, causing great loss of blood, a stroke, and partial paralysis. Whether the tiger, which had performed in the act for six years, attacked Roy or sought to drag him to safety by his neck after an accidental fall during the act remains a matter of dispute. Some witnesses thought the tiger, not knowing that Roy would not have thick skin around his neck as a tiger cub would, sought to help Roy, not to hurt him. Seriously wounded backstage, Roy said, "Don't hurt the cat." The show closed indefinitely.

With lions and tigers an integral part of their act, Siegfried and Roy established a breeding line of white tigers and lions, rescuing them from the brink of extinction. They actively support the College of Magic in Cape Town, South Africa with their SARMOTI (Siegfried and Roy, Masters of the Impossible) grant, enabling disadvantaged youth to enroll in the college and train to become professional magicians.

Roy's Mars, ruler of his Midheaven, is conjunct Spica in his fourth house, guiding him as an animal lover from a troubled home to international stardom. Neptune, opposing his Midheaven within one degree, is his Principal Planet, giving him the high sensitivity he needed to communicate with the big cats and his attraction to illusion. Neptune rules his 9th house, indicating that his success may be linked to other cultures. Virtually all of his success occurred outside his native Germany. Spica's placement in the 4th house illustrates a protective parent. Despite an alcoholic father and stepfather, Roy always maintained an excellent relationship with his mother, who moved into his Las Vegas mansion and managed it.

Chapter 8

THE CRITICAL 29TH DEGREE

*A man has no more character than he can
command in a crisis.*

ANONYMOUS

The 29th degree is the end of a zodiacal sign, or, for better or worse, the end of the line, or the end of the rope. Similar to a clock at 11:59 PM, it's the end of the proverbial 11th hour, a turning point that simultaneously marks an end and a beginning. It's a culmination of all previous degrees and thus all previous experiences so, like a train at the end of its journey, the 29th degree is the end of the sign and the beginning of another. It's perched to make a transition and, as a train in a station, changes occur when it reaches its destination. At the end of the line, announcements are made, passengers enter and depart, freight is loaded or unloaded, and the conductor changes the route of the engine. That particular journey has ended. An identical one may resume in a few minutes or a few days. It's the same, but different.

An adolescent graduates high school and goes to college. It's the same person, but they're at a turning point of their lives. So is the dutiful employee at their retirement dinner, or a recruit arriving at boot camp, or a refugee entering another country, or a woman giving birth. They're at the end of a line and are poised to pass into a new chapter of their lives. They're in transition.

Someone carrying their loved ones out of a burning building, or being rushed into a hospital emergency room, or stranded in foreign country, or coping (or not coping) with a catastrophe, is also at the end of the line. They're in crisis.

The end of one journey or experience is the beginning of another. Transition parlays into challenge. Crisis parlays into relief, or opportunity, or both. Either way, the end of the rope marks the beginning of another set of circumstances. And so it goes. We've all experienced crisis and transition in one form or another, but some people's lives are fundamentally characterized by them, either serving as a linchpin in a turning point or as someone who leads through crisis intervention, serving to close one chapter and open another. Individuals with a Principal Planet or Midheaven at 29 degrees have a tendency to disconnect—or be disconnected from—a trait or situation and embrace another wholeheartedly. A planet or angle at 29 degrees is like an inflated balloon; it's stretched to a point of culmination and is used to celebrate an occasion or turning point. When the party's over, the balloons are either burst in a loud "crisis" or, in the case of helium balloons, take wing and disappear. Either way, they've gone through a transition from their function as markers that commemorate turning points.

But they were a critical part of the journey.

An example of a chart with Midheaven at 29 degrees is the horoscope of Winston Churchill, shown as Chart 44.

Churchill was a British statesman, author, soldier, and the prime minister of Great Britain during World War II. His singular leadership and masterful rhetoric led Britons during their darkest hours of terror, striving against all odds to help them keep their stiff upper lip.

The son of Lord Randolph Churchill and American socialite Jennie Jerome, Winston Leonard Spencer Churchill

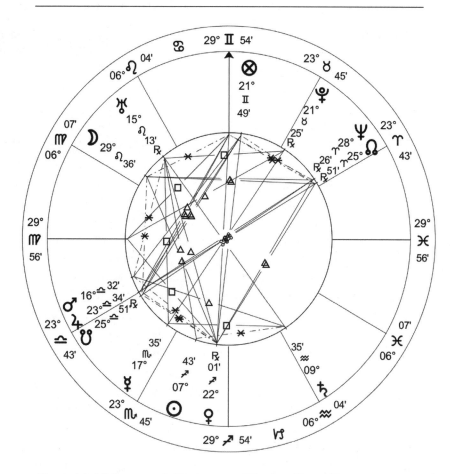

Chart 44. Midheaven at 29 degrees: Winston Churchill, November 30, 1874, 1:30 AM, GMT Woodstock, England, 51N52, 1W21.

was born two months prematurely in Blenheim Palace, after his mother suffered a horseback riding accident, resulting in lifelong delicate health. The oldest of two boys of a military dynasty, he was the direct descendant of John Churchill, who was named first Duke of Marlborough in 1702 for his victories against Louis XIV in the War of Spanish Succession. Growing up in the manor house that was built for Marlborough by the nation, Churchill's early childhood was marked by the aloof treatment he received from his parents. His father, Lord

Randolph wrote of him that he "lacked cleverness, knowledge and any capacity for settled work. He has a great talent for show-off, exaggeration and make-believe."[1] Contact with his mother, whom he loved dearly, was minimal. During his years at boarding school he wrote to her frequently begging her to either visit him or to allow him to come home. Replies were scant and impersonal. His primary caregiver was his beloved nanny, Elizabeth Anne Everest, whom he invited to visit him at school, shocking his wealthy classmates. One colleague noted years later that this act was "one of the greatest acts of courage and compassion he had ever seen."[2]

An undistinguished student, young Churchill earned high grades in English and history and was the school's fencing champion. In keeping with his military pedigree, he entered the Royal Military Academy at Sandhurst after two failed attempts. After graduation, he entered the army as a cavalry officer and war correspondent and participated in three military campaigns, the last in Sudan, in 1898, where he rode in what is described as the British Army's last cavalry charge at Omdurman. The 24-year-old imperturbable soldier proved well suited to the task. "I never felt the slightest nervousness," he wrote to his mother. "I felt as cool as I do now."[3]

Two years later, Churchill became a Member of Parliament. After a brief membership in the Conservative party, he switched allegiance and rose quickly through the ranks of the Liberal party, becoming Home Secretary in 1910 and First Lord of the Admiralty in 1911, a position that placed him on the world stage at the outbreak of World War I. He commissioned the plan to invade the Dardanelles, sending the army and navy to breach the defenses and capture Constantinople. The entire campaign was a tragic failure. Britain suffered a catastrophic defeat with over 140,000 troop losses, ultimately forcing Churchill's resignation and his subsequent political decline.

Returning to civilian life he rejoined the Conservative party in 1924 and was appointed as Chancellor of the Exchequer. His returning Great Britain to the gold standard proved financially disastrous for the country; Churchill later regarded this as the greatest mistake of his life. He stated he was not an economist and that he acted on the advice of the governor of the Bank of England. He further undermined his political position by opposing self-government in India, on the basis of his prediction that it would ultimately lead to bloodshed in India and mass unemployment at home. He resigned from office in 1931, appearing to enter, in his own words, his "wilderness years."

During this time Churchill focused on writing, including the biography of his ancestor, *Marlborough, His Life and Times* and *A History of the English Speaking Peoples*. Despite a low profile politically, his staunch anti-Nazi policy during these years strengthened his reputation and, after the resignation of Neville Chamberlain on May 10, 1940, King George VI immediately appointed Churchill as Prime Minister. On that same day, the German army invaded the Netherlands, Belgium, and Luxembourg, and two days later the Germans entered France. After France fell to the Nazis, England had no allies, leaving them open to the threat of German air attack, which inevitably began on July 10, 1940. The London Blitz sent the terrified population of Great Britain scrambling for shelter in underground bomb shelters, seeking guidance from their inspired war leader. Churchill's broadcasts on the BBC were their lifeline for hope: "We shall not flag or fail. We shall go on to the end. We shall fight in France, we shall fight on the seas and oceans, we shall fight with growing confidence and growing strength in the air. We shall defend our island, whatever the cost may be. We shall fight on the beaches, we shall fight on the landing-grounds, we shall fight in the fields and in the streets, we shall fight in the hills. We shall never surrender!"

After the bombing of Pearl Harbor on December 7, 1941, Churchill found an ally in President Roosevelt and the United States. Jubilant at the success of the D-Day invasion, Churchill earned the reputation of the greatest of all Britain's war leaders. A prolific writer throughout his life, he was awarded the Nobel Prize for Literature in 1953 for his epic six-volume series, *The*

Second World War. Historians refer to him as "The Man of the Twentieth Century."

Churchill married Clementine Ogilvy Hozier on September 12, 1908. The couple had five children. After a lifetime of battling depression, what he commonly referred to as "this black dog on my back," and surviving several strokes and heart attacks, Churchill died in his sleep on January 25, 1965.

• • •

An example of Midheaven Ruler at 29 degrees is shown in Chart 45, the horoscope of Randy Shilts.

Shilts is the American author of the 1987 bestseller *And The Band Played On,* the award-winning, groundbreaking book that chronicled the emergence of the AIDS epidemic in the United States. Translated into seven languages, the book was made into an HBO film in 1993 that won the Emmy Award for Outstanding Made-for-Television Movie.

A pioneering journalist, Shilts was an outspoken critic of much of the gay press, thinking it was more concerned with agenda than with unbiased reporting. Adamantly considering himself to be a reporter that happened to be gay as opposed to being a "gay reporter," he left no stone unturned to present an objective, gripping narrative of how a "gay disease" mushroomed into an epidemic due to the federal government placing budgetary concerns over medical treatment.

Growing up in the Chicago suburb of Aurora, Illinois, Shilts and his four brothers were raised in a solid Methodist family. His father, Bud, sold prefabricated housing and his mother Norma was a homemaker. After majoring in English at the University of Oregon at Eugene, he realized as he approached graduation that he was unable to write a declarative sentence. "Somebody told me you could learn grammar by taking a journalism course, so I took one and I just happened to be good at it."[4] Spending another year at the University, he became an award-winning editor of the student newspaper. Coming out publicly as a gay man at 20, he discovered he could not find a full-time job at a mainstream

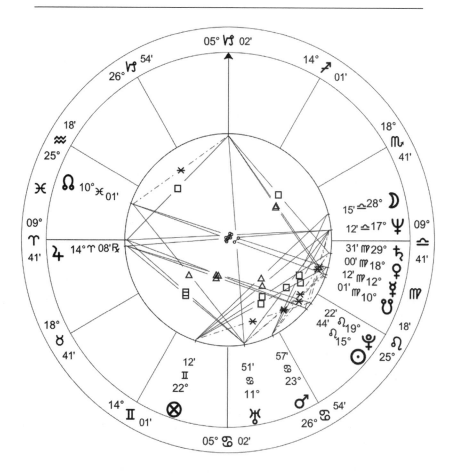

Chart 45. Midheaven Ruler at 29 degrees: Randy Shilts, August 8, 1951, 9:16 PM CST, Davenport, IA, 41N31, 90W34.

newspaper or radio station because of his sexual orientation. After struggling for several years as a free-lance journalist, he was hired at the *San Francisco Chronicle* in 1981 as a national correspondent, becoming "the first openly gay reporter with a gay 'beat' in the American mainstream press."[5] It was at this time that the Acquired Immune Deficiency Syndrome (AIDS), rampant in San Francisco, gained nationwide attention. In the epicenter of the crisis, Shilts immersed himself with reporting the medical, social, and political ramifications of the disease.

The result was his painstakingly researched opus, *And The Band Played On, Politics, People and the AIDS Epidemic,* which won the Stonewall Book Award and the 1988 Outstanding Author Award from the American Society of Journalists and Authors. Shilts' exposé of the controversial topic garnered international success. He wrote two other critically acclaimed books, *The Mayor of Castro Street: The Life and Times of Harvey Milk* (1982), and *Conduct Unbecoming, Gays and Lesbians in the U.S. Military: Vietnam to Persian Gulf* (1993).

As fate would have it, Shilts had symptoms of AIDS while writing *And The Band Played On,* but refused medical treatment thinking it would block his objectivity as a writer and reporter. He was found to be HIV positive in March, 1987, while writing the last pages of the book. Five years later, Shilts, homebound on oxygen, dictated the final pages of *Conduct Unbecoming* from his bed, finally disclosing his own case of AIDS.

He died on February 17, 1994, in Guerneville, California.

Saturn, the ruler of Shilt's Midheaven, is at 29 degrees Virgo in his 6th house of illness. His place in the world was characterized by a crisis (29 degrees), of an illness (Virgo, 6th house), that served as a turning point (29 degrees) in sexual and societal mores. Note that his Sun in Leo is exactly conjunct Cardinal Axis, which rules his 6th house. The AIDS pandemic is one of the most destructive epidemics in world history.

Chapter 9

THE EXPRESS LANE TO THE TOP

*Of all the possessions of this life fame is the noblest, when
the body has sunk into the dust the great name lives*

JOHANN VON SCHILLER

Famous people whose achievements reach across cultures and
who influence popular and political culture on a mass scale
attain astonishing success. They become the flagship icons of
following generations and their names are not only household
words, they are immortalized. In the Slevin System, the tried
and true formula that indicates success in one's chosen field of
endeavor is a specific aspect called the Boomerang. It occurs
when:

- The ruler of the Midheaven is in Ptolemaic aspect to
  the Midheaven.
- *Even if the ruler of the Midheaven is not the Principal Planet,* if it is conjunct, trine, sextile, square or
  opposing the Midheaven within an orb of 8 degrees,
  success is a given in the Slevin System.

In traditional astrology this particular aspect is know as "behold-ing," or within the line of vision. The planet can see or "behold" what it rules, in this case the Midheaven, producing a command-ing "boomerang" effect that fortifies and empowers. For exam-ple, let's take an imaginary chart with the Midheaven 17 degrees of Leo. Mars at 14 degrees Gemini is the Principal Planet and the Moon follows at 12 degrees Libra. Thus, in traditional terminol-ogy, Mars "beholds" the Midheaven first, followed by the Moon. In this imaginary chart, the Sun is at 25 degrees Scorpio, squar-ing the Sun. *Thus the Sun, ruler of the Midheaven, "beholds" the Sun-ruled Midheaven,* because it is within its line of vision, even if it is not the Principal Planet in this case. The Boomerang is designed to return to its point of origin, and so does the Mid-heaven Ruler aspecting the Midheaven, because *it shines its light back to the Midheaven, strengthening it exponentially.* Individu-als with this extremely fortunate aspect are poster people for suc-cess. In the style of an express elevator, Fate enables them to reach the top, parting obstacles like the Red Sea, and remain in a pent house of achievement. Their rank and public presentations can set the standard in their profession, and they often leave a legacy of notable success or notoriety. The allowable orb is 8 degrees on either side of the Midheaven.

Chart 46 provides an example of Midheaven Ruler square the Midheaven in the horoscope of Katharine Hepburn.

American actress and author, Hepburn was rated as the top female star in the Greatest American Screen Legends list. In a stellar career that spanned seventy years she received twelve Academy Award nominations for Best Actress and holds the record for most Best Actress awards, having won four. As a leading star of film, television, and the stage, she was interna-tionally known for her acerbic wit and rugged independence.

Hepburn was the second of six children of Dr. Thomas Nor-val Hepburn and Katharine Martha Houghton. Dr. Hepburn was a staunch pioneer against the spread of venereal diseases and mother Katharine, with her close friend Margaret Sanger, helped establish Planned Parenthood. The outspokenly liberal

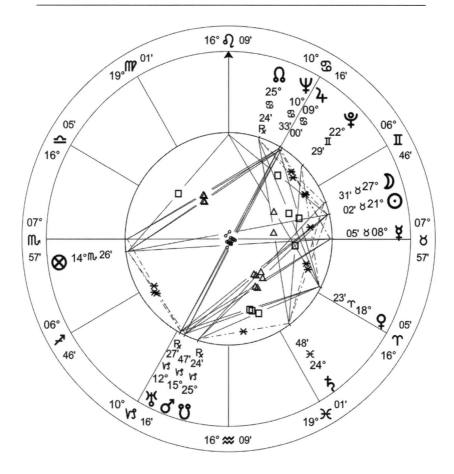

Chart 46. Midheaven Ruler square the Midheaven: Katharine Hepburn, May 12, 1907, 5:47 PM EST, Hartford, CT 41N46, 72W41

Hepburn family's dinner table discussions focused on these topics and other unorthodox subjects. All the children were encouraged to participate in these very adult conversations, and once young Hepburn accompanied her mother to a suffragette rally. Hepburn was very proud of her well to do, avant-garde family. "We were snubbed by everyone, but we grew quite to enjoy that."[1]

Insisting his children actively pursue athletics, Dr. Hepburn presided over lessons in golf, tennis, swimming, and any sport in which his children expressed an interest. Young Hepburn blossomed as a fine athlete, winning a bronze medal for figure skating, and entering the finals in the Connecticut Young Women's Golf Championship. Her marked athletic prowess empowered her to perform her own stunts in many later films, and she was an avid swimmer in her 80s. Yet despite her capacity to outdo anyone at any sport, she could never beat her beloved older brother Tom. In her attempt to be more boyish, she shaved her head every summer from age 9–13 and called herself Jimmy. When the Hepburn family was visiting an aunt in New York City, 13-year-old Hepburn found Tom hanged by the neck, dead, in the attic. It was never confirmed whether the death had been a suicide or a prank gone wrong, but the traumatized Hepburn nose-dived into depression, avoided friends, and was home schooled.

After graduating high school at Kingswood–Oxford School in Hartford, Hepburn attended Bryn Mawr College, where she smoked, drank, ignored curfew, and was known for her overall disregard for conventional behavior. A month before graduation she auditioned for a bit part in a Broadway show and was hired. On her graduation day, after receiving a degree in history and philosophy, Hepburn told her parents about her New York job on the stage and faced her father's fury and adamant disapproval.

Despite her adored father's reaction, Hepburn debuted on Broadway in the 1928 production of *Night Hostess*. That same year she married Ogden Ludlow Smith, a businessman she met at Bryn Mawr. Their marriage was problematic from the start. Hepburn spent the next four years working in small stock companies, finally earning a speaking role in the Broadway play *Art and Mrs. Bottle*. After being fired from several acting jobs the undaunted Hepburn was hired in 1932 to play an Amazon princess in the Broadway play *A Warrior Princess*, where Hepburn had to enter the stage by leaping down a staircase while carrying a large stag on her shoulders. A talent scout from RKO was in the audience. He was so impressed with Hepburn's physical prowess and performance of a freakish Amazon princess that he asked her to do a Hollywood screen test. The delighted Hepburn agreed and, after a Mexican divorce from Smith, she aced her screen test, demanding an outrageous salary of $1500 per week for the 1932 film *A Bill of Divorcement.* Impressed with her regal bearing, distinctive speech, and bold talent, she received it. The film was a hit, and so was Hepburn the following year in *Morning Glory,* winning the Academy Award. A series of flops followed, after which she was dubbed "box office poison." In 1940 her career revived almost overnight in the sensational Broadway play and film, *The Philadelphia Story.*

While filming *Woman of the Year* in 1942, Hepburn fell in love with costar Spencer Tracy, launching what would become one of Hollywood's most acclaimed romances, despite Tracy's marriage to another woman. The couple's dynamic chemistry blazed brilliantly in their nine films together and the relationship lasted until Tracy's death in 1967.

Off stage and screen Hepburn was known for her prickly personality, earning her the nickname "Katharine of Arrogance." Adamantly refusing to behave like a movie star, she refused to sign autographs, pose for pictures, or give interviews. Decades ahead of her time in fashion, she wore pants exclusively and no make-up. Shocked at her unconventional behavior, the public knowingly kept their distance.

Nominated for twelve Academy Awards over the course of her career, Hepburn won three, including *Guess Who's Coming to Dinner* (1967), *The Lion in Winter* (1968) and *On Golden Pond* (1981). In 1975 she won an Emmy for *Love Among the Ruins.* At age 77 she became a best selling author for her personal account of creating one of her best-known roles, *The Making of The African Queen,* and in 1991 published *Me,* her autobiography.

The tireless Hepburn retired at age 87 to her family home in Old Saybrook, Connecticut. She died of natural causes at age 96.

Venus, trining Hepburn's Midheaven with a tight orb of 2 degrees, 14 minutes, is Hepburn's Principal Planet, appropriately describing her pursuit of a career in the arts. However, the Sun, ruler of her creative Midheaven, is also square the Midheaven within 4 degrees and 52 minutes. Hepburn pursued her goal from her teens and, after her Oscar at age 26, she remained at the top for a stunning seventy-year career of unprecedented accolades.

• • •

Chart 47 provides an example of corulers of Midheaven aspecting Midheaven in the horoscope of Nicholas Culpeper.

English apothecary, botanist, herbalist, and author, Culpeper's *Complete Herbal*, first published in 1653, is the standard text in herbalism in the Western World and has been continuously in print for over 350 years.

Culpeper's father, Reverend Nicholas Culpeper, was presented with possession of Ockley Manor a few months prior to Nicholas' birth. His sudden death thirteen days prior to the birth of his son mandated that Ockley Manor pass into other hands. Culpeper's mother, Mary Attersole, brought her infant son to her maternal home in Isfield, where Culpeper grew up amid Mary and her parents, who were to have a profound effect upon their precocious grandson. Grandfather Reverend Attersole was a minister who presided over a Puritan congregation, and possessed a unique library of ancient literature. He taught his young grandson Latin and Greek in preparation for university and to follow in his own footsteps in a career in the ministry. On nature walks with Grandmother Attersole Culpeper learned the healing power of plants and wildflowers. Since he was only permitted to use his grandfather's library for reading the Bible and certain classical treatises, Culpeper squirreled away forbidden and obscure books, including a copy of Ptolemy's *Tetrabiblos,* and studied them in a hayloft. One was *Anatomie of Man's Body*, by Barber Surgeon Thomas Vicary, which had a picture of a human skeleton and a description of human reproduction. Thirteen-year-old Culpeper was permanently hooked.

A gifted scholar, at 16 Culpeper entered Cambridge University, his grandfather's alma mater, where he was to study the-

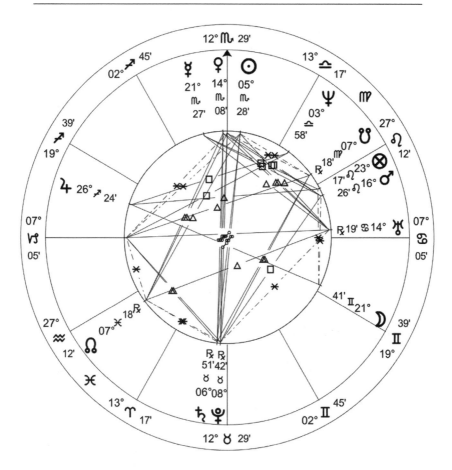

Chart 47. Midheaven Ruler aspecting Midheaven: Nicholas Culpeper, October 28, 1616, 12:12 PM LMT, Ockley, England, 51N09, 0W22.

ology for the ministry. During these salad days he squandered his entire paternal inheritance, neglected his studies, and fell in love with Judith Rivers, a childhood friend who was heir to a fortune. Knowing Judith's parents would never consent to the marriage, the couple planned to elope. The time and place were set, igniting a chain of events that transformed Culpeper from bon-vivant scholar to gifted healer.

Culpeper set out in a treacherous thunderstorm to meet his bride at the village of Lewes where the clandestine wedding was to take place. Judith was arriving in the opposite direction. As fate would have it, her coach was struck by lightning and she died instantly. Sir Nicholas Astey, a Cambridge friend of Culpeper's, was an eyewitness to this tragedy. Breaking the news, he escorted Culpeper, unbalanced in his grief, to his mother's home in Isfield where Culpeper suffered an acute nervous collapse. Emerging from this ordeal months later, he refused to return to Cambridge or enter the ministry, a decision that caused him to lose his maternal inheritance.

The final blow was Mary Attersole's own collapse from the stress of nursing her recalcitrant son. With her own health ruined, Mary died soon after Culpeper's recovery. Culpeper never fully recovered from these traumatic events, leaving him with episodes of depression, which were to plague him for the rest of his days. "I remember to have heard him confess that melancholy was an extraordinary enemy unto him; so great at sometimes, that wanting company he would seem like a dead man."[2]

Grandfather Attersole's connections reluctantly provided a position in London as an apprentice for an apothecary. Destitute yet delighted to finally study medicine, Culpeper displayed an outstanding aptitude as a "Student of Physick," excelling at several apprenticeships. In 1640 he married 15-year-old Alice Field, daughter of a well-to-do grain merchant, whose dowry Culpeper used to establish his own shop and home on Red Lion Street, Spitalfields, East London. It was here that Culpeper practiced the Art of Physick with astonishing skill. Possessing no business sense whatsoever, he preferred to treat the poor and charged them little or nothing at all. Treating up to forty patients a day with a high rate of success, he became London's best-known apothecary. Writing extensively in the evenings, he translated from Latin into English every extant herbal and medical text from antiquity to his present time, including one from the Aztecs in South America brought to Europe by a Spanish conquistador, compiling seventeen books in all. Among his greatest achievements were writing one of the first texts on obstetrics and completing the first English translations of *The Materia Medica* and *The Pharmacoepia*. The College of Surgeons made Culpeper an object of public derision for putting the knowledge of healing into the hands of the general public that could ill afford Latin-reading physicians.

With revolutionary zeal, Culpeper joined Lord Protector Oliver Cromwell on the Puritan side in the English Civil War, fighting in the Battle of Edgehill on October 23, 1642, and providing first aid on the battlefields. A bullet wound in his chest never completely healed, weakening his system and leaving him tubercular.

Culpeper lectured privately on medicine and linked horoscopes with health to an unusual and unprecedented degree. Illness was to be treated with respect and its cures to be revered with awe, as all cures hail from Dame Nature, whom Culpeper curiously refers to as his mother. "If you follow her you shall not want; she treads upon the world and looks upward. She always weeps, and yet I have never seen her laugh. We must know there is a sympathy between Celestial and Terrestrial bodies; which will easily appear, if we consider that the whole of creation is one entire and united body, composed by the power of an All-wise God, of a composition of discords."[3] Culpeper held that Dame Nature is the paintbrush of all creation and that her two sons, Dr. Reason and Dr. Experience, will lead a student of medicine on the road to truth. One can deduce from his writings that the human body is an imitation of nature and, nature, like the body, can only be compartmentalized with his microcosmic philosophy in mind. Above all, "a physitian [sic] without astrology is like a pudding without fat."[4]

The cornerstone of Culpeper's medical trade was the decumbiture, of which the literal definition is "the point of time of invasion of disease." To define this more clearly, the actual time of decumbiture occurs when one takes to his/her bed. The exact time is noted and horoscope is cast. This is the decumbiture, or chart of the illness. The cause, diagnosis, prognosis, and cure, or lack of one, are present in this chart and thereby most cautiously judged. A member of the Society of Astrologers, he was an acquaintance of master astrologer William Lilly. His masterpiece, *The Compleat Herbal and English Physician,* made him a legend in his own time. Along with the Bible and almanac it was packed in the British ships that sailed to the New World.

Culpeper's bouts of depression were deepened from continual illness within his own family. Alice bore him seven children and only one, a daughter, survived him. Wasted by tuberculosis, he died on January 10, 1654, at the age of 38.

Pluto, coruler of Culpeper's Midheaven, opposes his Midheaven within 11 minutes, and Mars, Midheaven coruler, squares the Midheaven with an orb of 7 degrees 55 minutes. The two corulers of the Midheaven in aspect to the Midheaven within an orb of 8 degrees paves an express route to the top with a legacy of wide-reaching influence and lasting recognition. The Nodes on the Cardinal Axis in Virgo and Pisces in the 8th and 2nd houses respectively, indicate Culpeper's connections to healing and philanthropy would place him on the world stage.

The powerful Boomerang aspect spreads its influence beyond Midheaven rulers aspecting Midheavens. It also works with Ascendant rulers aspecting Ascendants and when it does, success begins in childhood. These are the gifted and talented kids, whose precocious talents compel mentors to nurture and develop their superior abilities. Their early environment enables them to move up the ranks and they're often in the public eye as teenagers.

• • •

An example of Ascendant Ruler aspecting Ascendant is Chart 48, the horoscope of Tiger Woods.

Woods is an American professional golfer whose career on the green has been unprecedented. As the highest paid professional athlete in 2007 ($100 million), it is estimated he will be the first athlete in history to become a billionaire from winnings

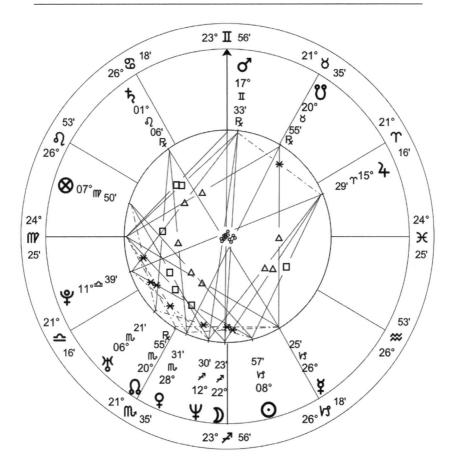

Chart 48. Ascendant Ruler aspecting Ascendant: Tiger Woods, December 30, 1975, 10:50 PM PST, Long Beach, California, 33N46 118W11

and endorsements. Awarded the PGA Tour Player of the Year eight times and Associated Press Male Athlete of the Year four times, he made history on April 13, 1997 as the youngest winner in the sixty-one-year history of the Masters Golf Tournament. His unmatched record includes winning the Masters four times, 1999 PGA Championship three times, the British Open three times and the US Open twice. His spectacular rise to the top coupled with his courtly demeanor and prodigious skill stupefied spectators across the globe.

Eldrick "Tiger" Woods is the only son of Earl and Kultida Woods. Earl, a retired U.S. Army lieutenant colonel and Vietnam War veteran, is 50 percent African American, 25 percent Chinese and 25 percent Native American. Kultida Punsawad, born in Thailand, is 50 percent Thai, 25 percent Chinese and 25 percent Dutch. Perhaps no other professional athlete can boast of such interracial diversity. He refers to his ethnic make-up as "Cablinasian" (a term he coined from Caucasian, Black, American Indian, and Asian).[5] A practicing Buddhist, he acquired his faith from his mother and has said it helps control his stubbornness and impatience. Woods has two half brothers and one half sister from his father's previous marriage.

A child prodigy raised in a supportive, loving family in Los Angeles, Woods began playing golf at age two. The following year he putted with Bob Hope on the Mike Douglas Show. By age five he appeared in *Golf Digest* and the television show *That's Incredible*. After winning the Junior World Championships six times, at age 15 he was voted Southern California Amateur Player of the Year and *Golf Digest* Amateur Player of the Year. After graduating Western High in Anaheim, Wood majored in economics at Stanford University, where he won his first collegiate event and was voted Pac-10 Player of the Year, NCAA First Team All-American and Stanford's Male Freshman of the Year, an award that encompasses all sports.

After two years of college, Woods turned professional in 1996, signing endorsement deals with Nike and Titleist worth $60 million combined. Named 1996 *Sports Illustrated* Sportsman of the Year and PGA Rookie of the Year, he won his first golf major the following April, the Masters, by a record twelve strokes, becoming the youngest winner ever and the first interracial one.

Training with coach Butch Harmon since 1992, Woods is known for his uncanny eye-hand coordination and laser focus. In his 1992 book *Training a Tiger*, father Earl writes that when Woods practiced as a child, Earl would shout, wave his arms, and run in circles to distract him, forcing Woods to immerse himself in his own zone of focus. A Buddhist, Woods meditated from youth, enhancing his legendary concentration. Despite a five-star income and jet-setting lifestyle, Woods is known for his easy-going manner and unpretentious personality. Actively involved in charity work, in 1996 Woods and his father Earl established The Tiger Woods Foundation, focusing on golf clinics for disadvantaged children, a grant program, and scholarships. In February 2006 Woods established The Tiger Woods Learning Center, an educational facility in Anaheim, California that includes year-round educational, sports, weekend, summer, and community outreach programs for grades four to twelve.

On October 5, 2004, Woods married Swedish model and former nanny Elin Nordegren. With residences in Barbados, Wyoming, and Sweden, home base is Jupiter Island, Florida. Their first child, a daughter, was born in June of 2007.

Mercury, Woods' Ascendant Ruler, trines his Ascendant with a 2-degree orb, indicating a high degree of success in a particular area in childhood. The Moon is conjunct his IC, indicating a hereditary influence can manifest in his public presentation. Woods' father Earl, who passed away on May 3, 2006, entered college on a baseball scholarship and was offered a professional contract.

• • •

The horoscope of Celine Dion, Chart 49 on page 178, provides an example of Ascendant Ruler aspecting Ascendant.

A French-Canadian singer who emerged from a local talent to an international success in three years, Dion is the most successful singer in the history of Canadian music. A five-time Grammy winner with a total of 220 million records sold worldwide, she ranks as one of the top-selling musicians of all time.

Dion, the youngest of fourteen children born to Ademar Dion and Therese Tanguay, was raised in a provincial Quebecois community. Despite great financial hardship, the extraordinarily loving family of seventeen (including Grandma), readily shared four bedrooms, one bathroom, and no modern conve-

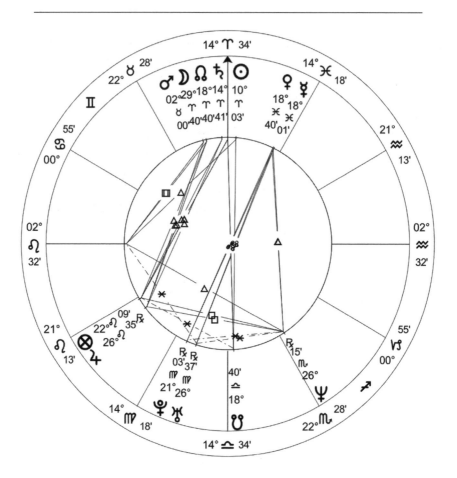

Chart 49. Ascendant Ruler aspecting Ascendant: Celine Dion, March 30, 1968, 12:15 PM EST Charlemagne, Quebec 45N43 73W29

niences. Both Ademar and Therese were professional musicians on the local circuit with several of their children making up their band. At the nightly family sing-alongs at the piano, four-year old Celine stunned her family with her four-octave range, and a year later she sang in public for the first time at her brother Michel's wedding. With a daughter, Ademar bought The Vieux Baril (The Old Barrel), a nightclub in Charlemagne, where little Celine unabashedly sang with her older siblings and other professional bands onstage, usually stealing the show, with the audience roaring for encores from the little girl with the amazing voice. They were never disappointed.

Astonished at her young daughter's exceptional musical ear, her outstanding vocal talent, and her prodigious ability to face and handle an audience, tireless Therese was determined to put Celine on the professional stage. After booking her at every local club and festival, she needed an agent for Montreal venues. Brother Michel, a professional musician, chose one from a record label named Rene Angelil and mailed a demo tape of Celine singing "It Was Only a Dream," a song Therese, Michel, and Celine composed. After hearing it, Angelil called the twelve-year-old chanteuse into his office, asking her to sing it in front of him. When Celine was finished, Angelil was in tears. He told her parents, "If you put your faith in me, I can guarantee your daughter will be an important star in Quebec and France within five years."[6]

Savvy Angelil wasted no time. He removed seventh-grader Celine, always an indifferent student, from school in order for her to record, tour, and make TV appearances in Quebec and France without interruption. After mortgaging his home to finance her first record in 1981, *La Voix du Bon Dieu* (*The Voice of God*), it hit number one on the Quebec charts, making her an instant star. By 1982 she was competing in the Yamaha World Popular Song Festival in Tokyo, Japan, and came in first in two categories, "Top Performer" and "Best Song." The following year she was the first Canadian to receive a gold record in France for the single "D'Amour Où D'Amitie" ("Of Love or Friendship"). Numerous Felix Awards honoring Quebecois artists followed, and by 1988 she had recorded fourteen albums to critical and popular acclaim. Her fate was sealed in 1988 when she won first place in the Eurovision Song Contest in Dublin, Ireland, viewed by over 600 million in Europe, Asia, and Australia. Recognition was yet to come in the U.S., however, because Celine sang only in her native French.

To successfully market her to an American audience, in 1989 the Svengali-like Angelil removed Celine from the spotlight and had her undergo a complete makeover. Orthodontists straightened her teeth, couturiers dressed her in high fashion, and makeup artists enhanced her face. Then came months at the École Berlet where Celine applied her legendary work ethic to learn to speak English fluently. Next stop, America, where in 1990 her first album in English, *Unison*, won rave reviews, and the single "Where Does My Heart Beat Now" hit the Billboard Hot 100 at number four. Established as a rising singer in the United States, her breakthrough came in 1991 with the recording with Peabo Bryson of the title track of Disney's animated film *Beauty and the Beast*, winning her a Grammy for Best Pop Performance.

At the top of her game in 1992, Celine's Quebecois fans criticized her for neglecting them, since she no longer sang in French. After winning Quebec's "English Artist of the Year," Celine reconnected with her first fans by openly refusing to accept the award, asserting that she was and always would be a French artist. The years of working and touring with manager Rene Angelil, twenty-six years her senior, culminated in his transition from mentor to lover in 1988, at 20-year-old Celine's instigation. Fearing possible bad press, they kept their relationship a secret for years. On December 17, 1994, they were married in a spectacular wedding ceremony in Montreal's Cathedral du Notre Dame.

Keeping to her French roots, Celine released French recordings between each English album, including *D'eux*, which became the best-selling French album of all time. Further recognition in America followed with blockbuster albums *The Colour of My Love* (1993), and *Falling Into You* (1996). Megastar status was achieved when she topped the charts worldwide in 1997 with the single "My Heart Will Go On," the theme from the blockbuster film *Titanic*, which became her signature song, winning her another Grammy for Record of the Year.

Despite a phenomenal career, a loving husband, and multiple homes, Celine lacked the one thing she longed for more than anything—a child. After a farewell concert on November

1, 1999, she withdrew from show business to attend to her husband's bout of throat cancer and begin a family. Angelil's low sperm count demanded Celine undertake intensive fertility treatment and, after successful artificial insemination, their son Rene-Charles was born on January 25, 2001.

On March 25, 2003, Celine opened her extravaganza floor-show "A New Day" at Las Vegas' Caesar's Palace in a four thousand-seat arena. It sold out nearly every night.

Never one to forget where she came from, Celine donates many of the proceeds of her Las Vegas show to charitable causes, notably Canadian Cystic Fibrosis, a disease that took the life of her beloved niece. At 18 she purchased a new home for her parents, and employs many of her siblings. "I'll be a Quebecker–Canadian. I'm from Quebec and every time I go to a country I say that. It's my roots, my origins and it's the most important thing to me."[7]

Celine Dion's Sun, ruler of her Ascendant, is exalted, conjunct her Midheaven, and trines her Ascendant with an orb of 7 degrees and 31 minutes, indicating a talent or trait that would manifest in childhood. Saturn, exactly conjunct her Midheaven within 6 minutes and thus her Principal Planet, illustrates a hereditary ability that influences her public presentation. The Moon, also in the 10th house, gives double emphasis to her "neon genes."

Chapter 10

AND FOR THE REST OF US

*The Genius of the United States is not best or most in its
executives or legislatures, nor in its ambassadors or authors or
colleges, or churches or parlors, nor even in its newspapers or
inventors, but always most in the common people.*

WALT WHITMAN[1]

Most of the horoscopes of successful people demonstrated throughout this book using the Slevin System are those who rank in the top five percent of their profession. Note that their horoscopes are well-integrated maps of well-aspected angles, prominent degrees, tight orbs, and angular planets, often with multiple elements of the Slevin System replicating themselves throughout their charts. These same components will also illustrate the route to success in the horoscopes of the general population that work in their chosen professions without front-page fanfare. Those who earn a high profile of recognition in a limited sphere of influence may be a big fish in a small pond without having their names on the proverbial front page. The

Slevin System works for everyday people just as it does for celebrities. The twelve steps can be implemented on any birth chart whatsoever.

Occasionally horoscopes present themselves that have no aspects to the Midheaven within eight degrees and thus no Principal Planet. Thus an alternate route to success is created. In these cases the Midheaven Ruler takes precedence, along with its house location and the Ptolemaic aspects it makes. While the Midheaven Ruler may describe the inclination toward a chosen profession, the lack of aspects to the Midheaven can make it difficult for them to access the equipment needed for their public presentation. They must find a way or make one through a labyrinth of professional possibilities to reach their summit. As in the fable of the stranded frog in the milk pail whose continuously flailing feet turn the milk into a solid piece of butter that enables him to climb over the top to freedom, these individuals can immerse themselves in a solitary pursuit and doggedly persist to their goal.

Chart 50 provides an example of Unaspected Midheaven in the horoscope of Carol McCrea.

McCrea is an American management consultant. Carol worked a series of odd jobs from age 13 for pocket money, while earning straight As through high school. Leaving home at 17, Carol received government grants to fund over six years of college, where she majored in pre-law, followed by graduate school, where again she earned perfect grades and graduated summa cum laude. Her love of animals, especially horses, led to a career in horse management at high profile racetracks and, along with establishing and managing chiropractic offices, led to the early use of chiropractic care for equines. Carol's financial support through various fields including corporate jobs, paralegal work, and eight years as a Naval Intelligence Officer allowed her to indulge in her true passion of extensive globetrotting.

Jupiter, coruler of the Pisces Midheaven, is exalted and conjunct Uranus in Carol's 2nd house, indicating financial lucky

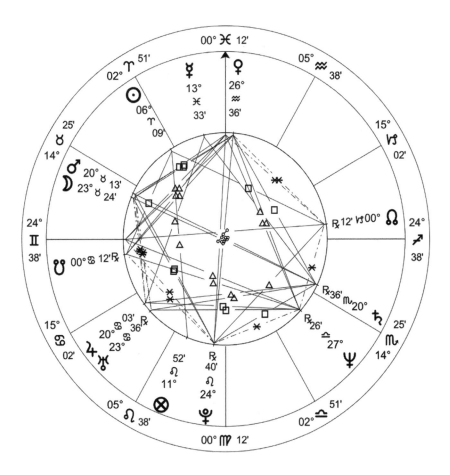

Chart 50. Unaspected Midheaven: Carol McCrea. March 27, 1955, 9:49 AM EST, Glen Ridge, NJ 40N49, 74W13

breaks. The Jupiter-Uranus conjunction squares Neptune, the other Midheaven coruler, in the fifth house, highlighting the eclectic and serendipitous circumstances that led to career employment and an unusual social life connected with the race track and celebrity athletes.

• • •

An example of Midheaven Ruler aspecting Midheaven is shown in the horoscope of an American commodities trader, Sean, Chart 51 on page 187.

Working independently from home on a laptop, Sean earns a living trading futures in markets around the globe. With a bachelor of science degree in engineering and a master's degree in science management, he worked as a corporate industrial engineer and telecommunications specialist, working on the team that developed the inertial navigation system used in the stealth bomber in the Gulf War. After losing his job through Reaganomics and trickle down, he decided to pursue his lifelong hobby of stock market trading.

Pluto, coruler of the Midheaven and his Principal Planet, squares the Midheaven within 6 degrees and 57 minutes, demonstrating the boomerang effect of success. The Moon in the 10th house serves as an indicator of passing down a family trait that is manifest in the public presentation. Sean's paternal grandfather was a grain trader in the British Isles in the nineteenth century and his father occasionally traded grains in the New York futures market.

• • •

Chart 52 on page 188 provides an example of Ascendant Ruler aspecting Ascendant.

An American athlete whose ability manifested in early childhood, John Slevin began wrestling on local teams in elementary and middle school, frequently winning first place. As a varsity wrestler in first year of high school, he trained intensively each summer with a Russian national wrestling champion in Belarus. By senior year he was two-time All American and won a wrestling scholarship to college. Mars at 11 degrees Aquarius sextiles his Mars-ruled Aries Ascendant within 6 degrees and 7 minutes, creating the boomerang effect to highlight an ability recognized

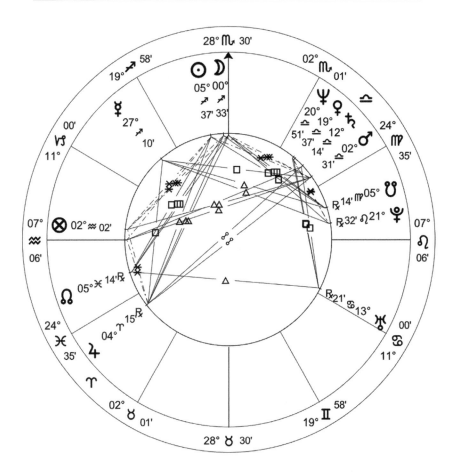

Chart 51. Midheaven Ruler aspecting Midheaven: Sean, November 28. 1951, 11:15 AM EST, Orange, NJ 40N46 74W14.

in childhood that propelled him into the spotlight. Noting a hereditary influence with the signs Capricorn and Cancer on the MC/IC axis, John's paternal grandfather was also a champion athlete.

• • •

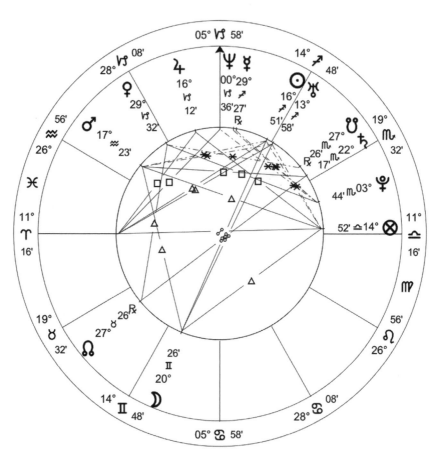

Chart 52. Ascendant Ruler aspecting Ascendant: John Slevin, December 8, 1984, 1:12 PM EST Newark, NJ 40N49, 74W13.

An example of Neptune as Principal Planet is shown as Chart 53 on page 189.

Lucy earned a bachelor of arts degree in psychology followed by a master's degree in painting. With a Virgo Midheaven and Mercury, Midheaven Ruler, in her 6th house, she graduated culinary school and worked for ten years as a professional chef. Eventually disliking the rigors and chain of command of corporate kitchens, she withdrew from working in the food

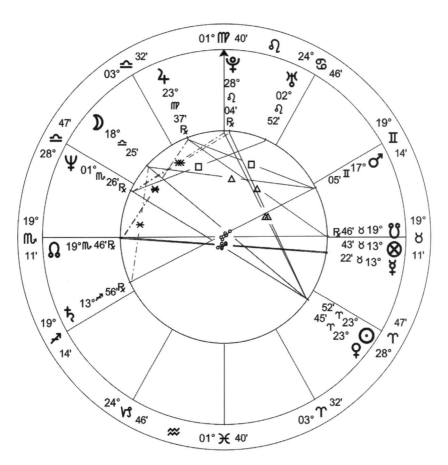

Chart 53. Neptune as Principal Planet: Lucy, April 13, 1957, 9:25 PM EST
Lansing, MI 42N43, 84W53

industry and started her own business as a professional painter, concentrating on murals and interior design (Neptune corules 4th house of homes), utilizing superb color coordination. Cultivating a creative lifestyle outside the mainstream, she enjoys living simply and supplements her income with astrology and tarot readings, utilizing down time to create through painting and writing.

EPILOGUE

The 12-Step Slevin System, with its conditions of success, has been presented in the horoscopes of superstars and everyday people. Well-aspected angles and prominent degrees replicate themselves like DNA patterns in birthcharts to highlight notable characteristics that place the individual in the public eye. So, dear reader, use the Slevin System. Find your Principal Planet and the best route to move the goods from the depths of your being to your best public presentation in the marketplace. And may success be your constant companion.

NOTES

CHAPTER 1

1. Clyde Farnsworth, *New York Times Magazine*, February 2, 1964.

CHAPTER 2

1. Helmut and Alison Gernsheim, *Victoria R* (New York: G. P. Putnam and Sons, 1959), p. 8.
2. *Time Magazine* cover, 1966.
3   *U.S. News and World Report*, September, 1997.
4. Interview with Kira Albin, 1997, *www.Grandtimes.com*.
5. Ibid.
6. William Butler Yeats, from "Sailing to Byzantium."
7. Stephen Holden, "Adrift from Pop, Billy Joel Takes a Classical Turn," *New York Times*, September 14, 1977.
8. *New York Times*, July 23, 2004, p. B 7.

CHAPTER 3

1. Donald E. Knuth, "Structured Programming with go to Statements," *Computing Surveys*, Vol. 6, No. 4, December 1974, p. 291.
2. "The Long Ride," Lucky Luciano, *http://www.crimelibrary.com/gangsters_outlaws/mob_bosses/luciano/ride_3.html*.
3. Alfred W. McCoy, Leonard P. Adams, Catherine R. Read, *The Politics of Heroin in Southeast Asia* (New York: Harper Collins, 1972).
4. As quoted at *http://www.springfield.k12.il.us/schools/southeast/bovary/middle*

5. "About Naomi," *http://www.naomijudd.com/about.php.*
6. Deidre Bair, *Jung, A Biography* (Boston: Little, Brown, 2003), p. 21.
7. Carl Jung, *Memories, Dreams, Reflections* (New York: Random House, 1965), pp. 30–31.
8. *Jung, A Biography,* p.115.
9. *Memories, Dreams, Reflections*, p. 106.

CHAPTER 5

1. Cecil Beaton, *Vogue* magazine, Alexander Walker. *Audrey, Her Real Story* (New York: St. Martin's Press, 1995), p. 8
2. Hepburn obituary, Caryn James, *New York Times*, January 21, 1993.

CHAPTER 6

1. "A Star is Reborn," Lynda Lee-Potter, *Weekend* Magazine, The *London Daily Mail,* 14 June 2003, republished at *http://www.lizaonline.co.uk.*
2. Ibid.
3. Ibid.
4. Pop Review, Stephen Holden, *New York Times*, June 3, 2002.
5 "Russian Revolution (1917)," *http://en.wikipedia.org/wiki/Russian_Revolution.*

CHAPTER 7

1. William Lilly, *Christian Astrology* (London: Regulus Publishing Co. Ltd. 1985 Reprint of 1647 edition), p.621.
2. Jackie Slevin, "Why Astrology Works," originally published in *Llewellyn's Sun Sign Book* (Woodbury, MN: 1995), p.383.
3. Sybil Leek, *My Life in Astrology* (New York: Signet, 1974), chapter 5.
4 "Francis Scott (Key) Fitzgerald (1896-1940)," *http://www.kirjasto.sci.fi/fsfitzg.*
5 Ibid.
6. "A Brief Life of Fitzgerald," *http://www.sc.edu/fitzgerald/biography.html.*

7. Ibid.

8. "Siegfried & Roy: Masters of the Impossible," *http://www.sieg-friedandroy.com/biograhy.*

CHAPTER 8

1 "Winston Churchill," *http://en.Wikipedia.org./wiki/Winston_Churchill.*

2 "Leaders & Revolutionaries: Winston Churchill," John Keegan, *http://www.time.com/time/time100/leaders/profile/churchill.html.*

3. "Winston Churchill," *http://logos_endless_summer.tripod.com/id126.html*

4. "Randy Shilts, 1951-1994," by Janice Albert, *www.cateweb.org/CA_Authors/shilts.htm.*

5. *"The Mayor of Castro Street: The Life and Times of Harvey Milk* by Randy Shilts" quoted on *http://www.queertheory.com/histories/s/shilts_randy.htm*

CHAPTER 9

1. "Katharine Hepburn," *www.wikipedia.org/wiki/Katharine_Hepburn.*

2. John Gadbury, *A Collection of Nativities* (London, 1661. Ballantrae Reprint, Universe Books, Ontario, Canada), p. 141.

3. Nicholas Culpeper, *Astrological Judgment of Disease.* (London, 1655. Ballantrae Reprint. Universe Books, Ontario, Canada), p. 68.

4. Nicholas Culpeper, *Astrological Judgment of Disease* (London, 1655. Ballantrae Reprint, Universe Books. Ontario, Canada), p. 48.

5. "Tiger Woods," *en.wikipedia.org/wiki/tiger_woods*

6. Celine Dion, *My Story, My Dream* (NY: Harper Collins, 2000), p. 58.

7. "Celine Dion," *en.wikipedia.org/wiki/Celine_dion.*

CHAPTER 10

1. Walt Whitman, *Democratic Vistas* (Washington, D.C.: J.S. Redfield, 1871).

LIST OF CHARTS

Alexandra, Czarina of Russia, 134

Neil Armstrong, 34

Joan Baez, 110

Brigitte Bardot, 23

Clara Barton, 31

Louis Braille, 20

Julia Child, 45

Winston Churchill, 159

Nicholas Culpeper, 171

Marie Curie, 25

Dalai Lama XIV, 37

Diana, Princess of Wales, 150

Celine Dion, 178

Elizabeth II, Queen of England, 60

Amy Fisher, 70

F. Scott Fitzgerald, 146

Gustave Flaubert, 93

Steve Forbes, 132

Diane von Furstenberg, 90

Galileo Galilei, 57

Al Gore, 76

Grace, Princess of Monaco, 18

Che Guevara, 64

Audrey Hepburn, 119

Katharine Hepburn, 167

Thor Heyerdahl, 28

Roy Horn, 153

Billy Joel, 51

Naomi Judd, 96

Carl Jung, 102

John F. Kennedy, 83

Jack Kerouac, 13

Sybil Leek, 143

Jay Leno, 140

"Lucky" Luciano, 79

Christa McAuliffe, 99

Carol McCrea, 185

Liza Minelli, 129

Benito Mussolini, 113

Shaquille O'Neal, 122

Norman Schwarzkopf, 9

Randy Shilts, 163

Curtis Sliwa, 54

Steven Spielberg, 87

Donald Trump, 11

Victoria, Queen of England, 43

Raoul Wallenberg, 67

Simon Wiesenthal, 16

Tiger Woods, 175

William Butler Yeats, 48

ABOUT THE AUTHOR

Jackie Slevin M.A., C.A. NCGR, has acted as Co-Director of Education of The National Council for Geocosmic Research (NCGR), being the Dean and Founder of the University of Geocosmic Studies. A professional teacher, lecturer and consultant for over 20 years, her articles on astrology have been published internationally. A graduate of the course in Classical Studies in Horary, Jackie served as the NCGR representative for the UAC 2002 Education Committee. She lives in Montclair, New Jersey. For more information, visit her website at *www.geocosmicstudies.com*.